THE DEVELOPMENT
OF DOCTRINE
IN THE CHURCH

THE DEVELOPMENT OF DOCTRINE IN THE CHURCH

by
Peter Toon

WILLIAM B. EERDMANS PUBLISHING COMPANY
GRAND RAPIDS, MICHIGAN

For
Albert H. Freundt, Jr.
who has personified for me
"Southern" kindness and hospitality

Library of Congress Cataloging in Publication Data

Toon, Peter, 1939-
    The development of doctrine in the church.

    Includes index.
    1. Dogma, Development of.   2. Theology, Doctrinal—
History. I. Title.
BT21.2.T66 1979   230   78-31490
ISBN 0-8028-1787-4

CONTENTS

PREFACE

MY INTEREST in the development of doctrine was first stimulated by membership in a study group on Scripture and tradition attached to Latimer House, Oxford. It was increased through a similar study group of the Tyndale Fellowship, based in Cambridge. I have lectured on the subject in several seminaries in the United States: Reformed Seminary, Jackson; Trinity Evangelical Divinity School, Deerfield; and Covenant Seminary, St. Louis—as well as at Western Kentucky University.

Thus, what I present here, while being my own thoughts, represents also what I have learned from colleagues and students. In particular, I would like to thank James I. Packer, David F. Wright, Richard Bauckham, Arvin G. Vos, James D. Spiceland, Paul Helm, Jeffrey Steenson, Jack Rogers, and Roger T. Beckwith.

My presentation is not meant to be definitive. Rather, it is meant to be gently provocative, inviting my evangelical friends to consider the whole subject of development of doctrine in the Church of our Lord and Savior, Jesus Christ.

Mrs. Eunice Thorpe helped me with the typing.

Peter Toon
Oak Hill Anglican
Theological College
London, England

INTRODUCTION

ALL CHRISTIANS CLAIM that their faith is based ultimately on Holy Scripture. God has revealed himself through words and deeds and primarily in the person and work of Christ. This revelation is recorded in Holy Scripture and by it Christians form their theology and guide their lives.

Most Christians belong to churches or denominations which claim to be tied to a system of doctrine based on Scripture and set forth in creeds, confessions of faith, and articles of religion. Lutherans have their Augsburg Confession, Anglicans their Thirty-Nine Articles, Presbyterians their Westminster Confession, Roman Catholics their conciliar decrees and papal pronouncements, and Baptists have their differing creedal statements. Also, many Christian colleges and organizations have their statements of faith; perhaps the best known is that of the Inter-Varsity movement (now called U.C.C.F. in the United Kingdom).

Most churches and denominations also claim that they accept the Catholic creeds: the Apostles', Nicene, and Athanasian, which were produced before modern denominational divisions. Sometimes the teaching of these creeds is incorporated into a denominational confession of faith, while in other cases the creeds are specifically referred to as statements which are to be accepted (see Article VIII of the Thirty-Nine Articles).[1]

These creeds are composed of several fundamental Christian doctrines—for example, that Jesus Christ is truly the Son of God and that God is a Trinity of the Father, Son, and Holy Spirit. These doctrines can truly be called dogma, for they are accepted by the Christian Church throughout the world. Whether we call the specific Lutheran or Presbyterian or Anglican doctrines dogma is actually a matter of taste. To Lutherans of the seventeenth century, the doctrine of consubstantiation was dogma—but to Anglicans and Presbyterians it was merely a doctrine which they could not accept. Traditionally, Roman Catholics have referred to their official doctrines as dogma; for example, by the papal pronouncement of 1950 the doctrine of the Assumption of the Blessed Virgin Mary became a dogma for Roman Catholics. So as not to confuse the reader I shall use the term dogma only for the doctrines approved by the ecumenical councils of the first five centuries and I shall use the term doctrine to cover both the confessional teaching of churches and denominations as well as the teaching of individual theologians belonging to these.

Though rival doctrinal systems or interpretations were known in the Western Catholic Church before the sixteenth century (e.g., Anselm's and Abelard's different doctrines of the Atonement), it was only after the religious upheaval and revival of the Reformation that rival confessions of faith became a permanent feature of Christendom. Through missionary activity by the divided Church the differing confessions have been exported to most parts of the world. Further, as Protestantism has continued to produce new branches, such as the Pentecostal Church, the number of confessions has increased. So today we have many confessions and statements of faith, all claiming to summarize or

1. I recognize that neither the Reformers nor modern-day Christians interpret clauses or phrases of the early creeds in the same way as those who first wrote or used them. I am thinking of such expressions as "he descended into hell" and "the communion of the saints." See further J. N. D. Kelly, *The Early Christian Creeds* (1963).

expound accurately biblical teaching.

To the historian the emergence of these various systems of doctrine can be a fascinating study. Personally, I have always enjoyed studying the way in which the doctrine contained in the Westminster Confession of Faith (1647) evolved and also how, as modified by Congregational divines, it was set forth in the Savoy Declaration (1658) some eleven years later. Obviously each confession, be it a sixteenth- or a twentieth-century production, has been produced by particular men in specific circumstances. To understand the doctrine of the confession, why it is presented in a certain way, why it attacks certain errors and puts matters one way and not another, the historian has to explore in some detail and depth the full circumstances—religious, cultural, and political—surrounding its composition.

Often, after he has completed his work, the historian has shown that the writers of a confession were sincere and able men, yet men of a particular persuasion, with very definite views, and views often hardened by controversy. In their sincere attempts to formulate doctrine these workers were wearing, as it were, tinted spectacles—tinted by their own strongly held presuppositions. Thus, they tended to see in Scripture only that which their spectacles allowed them to see. So, for example, we can predict that if an Anglo-Catholic theologian sits down to write a chapter for a confession on the doctrine of the ministry he is going to teach a doctrine of the apostolic succession of bishops. This simple explanation of tinted spectacles is certainly not a complete answer to the question: "Why are there so many different confessions and doctrines?" but it certainly points in the right direction.

But does the same observation apply to the dogma of the Catholic creeds? The answer has to be a qualified yes. The framers of these creeds, especially the Nicene Creed, were men who spoke Greek and made use of Greek philosophical terminology. Their spectacles were thereby tinted. However, they spoke for the universal Church, not a denomination, and therefore their doctrines have the added weight that they are the confession of the Catholic Church, not a mere part of it. Having affirmed this, we have to admit that because of the famous disagreement over the procession of the Holy Spirit (cf. the *filioque* clause added to the Nicene Creed in the West) the dogma of the Nicene Creed is received in different ways in the Western and Eastern halves of Christendom.

Thus, in reiteration, there are basic facts which are necessary to the exploration of the development of doctrine. The first fact is Holy Scripture, the ultimate and final authority. In the case of some Christians, Holy Scripture will include the Apocrypha. The second is the Catholic creeds. The third is the existence of a wide variety of confessions of faith produced by the variety of denominations which make up the Catholic Church. The fourth is the life and history of the Church in which the doctrinal formulations took place.

What, then, is meant by the development of dogma or the development of doctrine? First, let us note what is not meant. Development of doctrine is not another term for the history of doctrines, as for example that provided by Louis Berkhof in his *The History of Christian Doctrines* (1937). Neither is it merely the history of a particular doctrine, for example, the doctrine of the Atonement. Rather, the development of doctrine takes for granted the histories of doctrines and seeks to answer particular questions which arise from the histories—questions such as: What is the relation of a particular doctrine to the Bible or biblical material on which it is based? What is the relation of a specific doctrine formulated in a later century to the "same" doctrine formulated in an earlier century—such as the doctrine of predestination in the sixteenth-century Reformed Confessions and the Westminster Confession of 1647? What is the relation between doctrine formulated in one language and culture and the "same" doctrine expressed later in a different language? And, what criteria can be established to test the emergence of doctrine so that it is possible to distinguish between "erroneous" and "faithful" expositions of doctrine?

Most histories of doctrine address one or more of these questions. In his justly famous *History of Dogma,* Adolf von

Harnack included a view of the development of dogma and made strong assertions about the relation of the doctrines of the Nicene Creed to the teaching of Scripture. More recently, Jaroslav Pelikan, who is very conscious of the problem of development, entitled his *magnum opus, The Christian Tradition: A History of the Development of Doctrine.* So, while it is possible to write a history of a doctrine without facing all the questions involved in the problem of development, those who would address themselves to the problem of development have to be aware of the histories of doctrines.

The problem of the development of doctrine is a comparatively new problem for theologians.[2] Christians in medieval and Reformation times were conscious of the fact that certain doctrines were not expounded by the Church until many years after the apostolic period. Their most common explanation for this phenomenon was that it was not necessary in the earlier period to make the proper logical deductions from the axioms provided by Scripture or by Catholic dogma. In other words, controversies had not raised questions to be answered and the implications of the worship and faith of the Church had not been fully recognized. When referring to the emergence and acceptance of "erroneous" doctrines, the Reformers referred to the "fall of the Church."[3]

The book generally used to trace the modern identification and first attempt to solve the problem of development is *An Essay on the Development of Christian Doctrine* (1845) by John Henry Newman. In the mid-nineteenth century the word "development" was commonly used in educated circles. People were conscious of the achievement of Western man in science, technology, exploration, trade, and the arts; thus, the history of culture, thought, and theology was rep-

2. Certain theologians of the early Church were conscious that they were "developing" doctrine. For Gregory of Nazianzus see J. Stevenson, *Creeds, Councils and Controversies* (Naperville, IL: Allenson, 1966), p. 59, and for Hilary see M. Wiles, *The Making of Christian Doctrine* (New York: Cambridge Univ. Press, 1967), pp. 32–33.
3. See further F. H. Littell, *The Origins of Sectarian Protestantism* (New York: Macmillan, 1964), pp. 46–78.

resented as a development—a progression in both quantity and quality.[4] Naturally, therefore, the word "development" remained as the key term whenever there was a discussion of the relation of later to earlier doctrine. And the word is still with us, even though we may think it is no longer the best possible word!

Significantly, Newman's book was written as the modern "scientific" study of history was beginning and as Newman sought to convince himself that his desire to leave Anglicanism for the Church of Rome was based on solid theological convictions. Since the appearance of the book, now regarded as a classic, the problem still exists. As indicated by an abundance of literature, it has been and is an *acute* problem for Roman Catholics. For many Protestants the problem is often stated relative to the difficulties in interpreting Scripture (hermeneutics) or in the relation of Scripture and tradition. For evangelical Protestants the problem appears not to have been discussed as much in recent decades as it was in the period from 1845 to 1914.

Thus, in this book I address myself to fellow evangelicals, particularly to students of theology in universities and seminaries. At the same time I hope that Christians who are not evangelicals will do me the honor of reading what I have to say. Apart from the obvious intellectual value of studying the problem of the development of doctrine, it is my conviction that awareness of the problem will help us relate to thinkers from other Christian traditions as well as make us better teachers of doctrine.

I begin with an account of Newman's *Essay* and then describe in some detail three specific responses to it by three leading Protestant theologians—Mozley, Cunningham, and Rainy. This historical account will help us to see how the problem was posed and answered in the middle of the Victorian era. Then, after a brief account of the way in which Harnack presented the development of dogma, I shall describe a further evangelical Protestant portrayal of de-

4. See further Michael Foucault, *The Archeology of Knowledge,* trans. A. M. Sheridan-Smith (New York: Irvington, 1972).

velopment, that by James Orr, which was a response both to Newman and Harnack.

Having brought my reader into the twentieth century, I shall indicate how Roman Catholics have confronted this acute problem and also how Protestants have indirectly confronted it in their discussion of Scripture, tradition, and hermeneutics. In the final chapter I shall offer criteria by which specific developments of doctrine can be evaluated.

To those with roots in one or other of the German or Dutch Churches of the nineteenth century, I apologize for not having included one or more chapters on evangelical views of development in German or Dutch literature. I suspect that in connection with the large number of histories of doctrine which were produced in Germany in the nineteenth century, evangelicals did much thinking about the development of doctrine. Yet, since I do not have the competence to examine this possibility and since, as far as I can ascertain, there are no good secondary books on the topic, I have had to abandon it to be studied and written up by someone else. However, I would commend Jaroslav Pelikan's *Historical Theology: Continuity and Change in Christian Doctrine* (1971), for the valuable information it supplies on Germanic views, and I would add that I have devoted several pages to the views of Adolf von Harnack.

Finally, may I say that some students may find this book more useful if they read chapters five and seven before they read chapters one to four and six. It is hoped that chapters five and seven will help enlighten them to the *problem* of development of doctrine and, therefore, give them more appreciation for the contributions of theologians of the past.

CHAPTER ONE

THE THEORY OF JOHN HENRY NEWMAN

JOHN HENRY NEWMAN died in 1890 as a Cardinal of the Roman Catholic Church. This seems remarkable when it is recalled that at the age of fifteen, in 1816, he professed to have an evangelical conversion. Between this evangelical experience and his entering the Church of Rome in 1845, there is a fascinating and complex religious and theological pilgrimage—a pilgrimage described in his famous autobiography, the *Apologia Pro Vita Sua* (1864) and interpreted in various ways by his biographers.[1] For our purposes, I have selected material from this pilgrimage which helps us to understand his joining the Roman Church and, more particularly, the justification he supplied for this in the *Essay on the Development of Christian Doctrine* (1845).

The Adoption and Later Abandonment of Evangelicalism

From the human viewpoint, the origins of a serious commitment to God and to Christian dogma in the life of Newman are related to his external circumstances in 1816. In March of that year the London bank, in which Newman's father was a partner, collapsed in the financial crisis follow-

1. Two of the better biographies are Meriol Trevor, *Newman's Journey* (London: Fontana, 1974) and C. S. Dessain, *John Henry Newman,* 2nd ed. (Stanford: Stanford Univ. Press, 1971).

ing the Napoleonic wars. It is difficult accurately to determine whether or not the worry about this contributed to his subsequent illness in early summer, but he remained at his boarding school to convalesce during the summer holidays. It was during this period that he came under the personal influence of Walter Mayers, a young evangelical clergyman who taught at the school in Ealing, near London. Newman later referred to Mayers "as the human means of the beginning of divine faith in me."[2] Not only did Mayers commend to the young Newman the evangelical understanding of faith and conversion, but he also put into his hands the writings of Thomas Scott, a leading evangelical clergyman whose commentary on the Bible was read in many homes. Scott's writings "made a deep impression on my mind," said Newman.[3]

About a year after this conversion experience Newman entered Trinity College, Oxford. After earning his Bachelor of Arts degree he became a Fellow and Tutor of Oriel College in 1822. In the learned and challenging company of his colleagues, Newman's evangelical faith was modified and extended. From Edward Hawkins (later to become Head of the College) he learned to consider seriously the doctrine of baptismal regeneration, a doctrine traditionally favored by Anglican High Churchmen, but generally rejected by evangelicals. Also from Hawkins he learned to see the dangers involved in the exercise of private judgment (private, insulated interpretation of the Scriptures) and the need to explain and interpret the Bible by the best tradition of the Church. In other words, the Church was to teach doctrine by her formularies and to prove them by Scripture.

Newman's interest in the Caroline divines of the Church of England—Lancelot Andrewes, Jeremy Taylor, and William Laud, for example—was stimulated by other colleagues: John Keble, Hurrell Froude, and Edward B. Pusey, who later became his bosom friends.[4] To this period of the 1820s must also be traced two of Newman's

2. *Apologia* (London: Fontana, 1972), p. 100.
3. *Ibid.,* p. 98.
4. Trevor, *Newman's Journey,* pp. 25ff. and Dessain, *John Henry Newman,* pp. 8ff.

lifelong commitments. First, there was his love for the writings of the Church Fathers of the first five centuries, particularly the Alexandrian Fathers. His first major book, *The Arians of the Fourth Century,* treated Athanasius as a hero. Secondly, there was his committed opposition to what was then called liberalism and latitudinarianism. He opposed the viewpoint, which he found in his own college in the teaching of such men as Thomas Arnold (later Headmaster of Rugby) and Richard Whateley (later Archbishop of Dublin), which stated that Church dogma was not of primary importance and that the Bible was to be interpreted according to the laws of reason. Though he knew little about the system, he also opposed the "neology" (rationalist theology) of German writers. So by the early 1830s we find that Newman is no longer an evangelical. Though still regarding the enjoyment of personal fellowship with God as of supreme importance, he has incorporated into his thinking the doctrines of baptismal regeneration and the view that the Bible is to be interpreted according the unanimous testimony of the early, undivided Church. The implications of the latter included a very high view of the sacraments, of episcopal succession and of other related doctrines, which to the typical evangelical seemed to be akin to Roman Catholicism.

The Tracts for the Times

The motivation behind the famous publications known as the *Tracts for the Times,* which were produced by Newman and his friends between 1833 and 1841, cannot be understood apart from the general political and religious scene.[5] Following revolution in Europe, the British Parliament, which effectively controlled the Church of England and Ireland, decided to open its doors to all elected members, even if their known beliefs were contrary to those of the National Church. Then, as it were, to add insult to injury many proposals from nonconformists and liberals were published which outlined plans to reform the Church in its

5. R. W. Church, *The Oxford Movement* (Chicago: Univ. of Chicago Press, 1970). Reprint of 1891 edition.

organization, economics, and even doctrine. As the problems of Ireland were always pressing, the government decided to interfere directly in the Protestant Church of Ireland by abolishing various bishoprics, an act which outraged orthodox Churchmen. The effect of all this on Newman was to increase his commitment to what he believed were the truths of divine revelation. "Great events," he wrote, "were happening at home and abroad, which brought out into form and passionate expression the various beliefs which had so gradually been winning their way into my mind." John Keble, too, felt very strongly about the plight of the Church, and he preached on 14 July 1833 the famous "Assize Sermon" at Oxford on "The National Apostasy," which Newman, diminishing his own influence, called the beginning of the Oxford Movement. A little later, following a meeting of concerned friends, the *Tracts* began to appear. The authors, led by Newman, asserted the independence of the Church, which was a divine society, and not a mere department of State. They emphasized the apostolic succession, the great value of the sacraments, the value of fasting and penance as well as the need for prayer and humility. As Newman later explained:

> From beginnings so small, from elements of thought so fortuitous, with prospects so unpromising, the Anglo-Catholic party suddenly became a power in the National Church, and an object of alarm to her rulers and friends. Its originators would have found it difficult to say what they aimed at of a practical kind: rather, they put forth views and principles for their own sake, because they were true, as if they were obliged to say them; and, as they might be themselves surprised at their earnestness in uttering them, they had as great cause to be surprised at the success which attended their propagation. ... In a very few years a school of opinion was formed, fixed in its principles, indefinite and progressive in their range; and it extended itself into every part of the country. ... And so it proceeded, getting stronger and stronger every year, till it came into collision with the Nation, and that Church of the Nation, which it began by professing especially to serve.[6]

Many Churchmen supported the *Tracts* because they saw in them a ray of hope and because they did not see in them, at

6. *Apologia*, p. 153.

first, the principles which tended to overthrow the principles of the English Reformation.

The final, famous *Tract 90,* published in February 1841, attempted to explain the *Thirty-Nine Articles of Religion,* the Church Confession of Faith, in such a way as to condone seeming Roman Catholic views of the sacraments and tradition. This tract was condemned by the University of Oxford and by the Bishops of the Church. Newman took this condemnation as a sign that he should withdraw from active teaching within the Church, and he preached his last sermons as an Anglican minister in 1843. He moved out of the city to live in Littlemore, where he had built a small semi-monastic establishment. Here, with the spires of his beloved Oxford in the distance, he devoted nearly nine hours a day to study of the Fathers and translation of the works of Athanasius. In addition, he gave four hours to prayer and lived a life of discipline and penance. On 9 October 1845, he was received into the Church of Rome at Littlemore, by Fr. Dominic Barberi, an Italian Passionist, who first met Newman in 1844. Not long afterwards appeared *An Essay on the Development of Christian Doctrine,* a book on which he had been working for a year, and his friends and foes were able to read his apologetic for the Church of Rome.[7] Before examining the general contents of this now famous book, let us note what may be regarded as the preparation for its novel thesis in the earlier thinking of Newman.

Views on the Relation of Scripture and Dogma Prior to 1845

During the 1830s Newman, on several occasions, expounded his views on the relation of Scripture and tradition. ("Tradition" here means the doctrinal, liturgical, and ceremonial expressions of the early Church.) Newman's views may be understood under three aspects. The first aspect was a tradition which interprets Scripture. Here he had in mind the consensus of the teaching of the early Fathers; stated differently, it was the application of the famous Rule of St.

---

7. The best examination of the *Essay* is that by N. Lash, *Newman on Development* (Shepherdstown, WV: Patmos Press, 1975).

Vincent of Lérins—*quod ubique, quod semper, quod ab omnibus creditum est.*[8] The use of tradition as the interpreter of Scripture saved the Church from the insulated private judgment of individuals. Second, there was a tradition independent of Scripture, but which was confirmed by Scripture and in harmony with the principles of Scripture. Here Newman had in mind such matters as the practice of infant baptism and the meeting for worship on the Lord's Day and not on the Sabbath. Third, there was a tradition concerning discipline, customs, ceremonies, and historical facts—for example, the date of Easter and Christmas. At this stage of his thinking Newman specifically rejected the Roman Catholic claim that doctrine may rest on tradition, without specific Scriptural foundation.

A further important distinction made by Newman in this period (and maintained in the *Essay on Development*) was the division of tradition into two types, the episcopal and the prophetic. By episcopal tradition he meant the creeds; that is, the summaries of apostolic teaching essential for salvation, which were preserved in the local churches and passed on from one bishop to the next, and also shown to other churches as proof of orthodoxy. It is well known that in the first three or four centuries of the Church there was a variety of local creeds, which in their diversity also possessed an inner harmony. If episcopal tradition was a specific doctrinal tradition of central doctrines and facts, prophetic tradition was much wider and was a term used by Newman to describe the whole, ongoing life of the Church, including worship patterns, doctrines, customs, and decrees of Councils.

The mature expression of Newman's Anglican position on tradition is in his *Lectures on the Prophetical Office of the Church* (1837). A year later there were signs that his position was beginning to change. In Tract 85, entitled *Scripture*

---

8. Vincent of Lérins, who died before 450, was the author of the *Commonitorium* which is available in translations by C. A. Heurtley and T. H. Bindley. His canon, "the Vincentian Canon," has been very influential in both Roman Catholicism and Anglicanism, and is "What has been believed everywhere, always and by all."

and the Creed, he made use of the analogy of the seed and its growth, comparing the fundamental principles and teaching given in Scripture (which he called "seeds of thoughts") with what happens to the seed in the life of the Church—that is, it grows into dogma or the teaching of the creeds. This new concept of tradition as organic growth was expounded by Newman in the fifteenth sermon he preached before the University of Oxford.[9] He preached from Luke 2:19 and 2:51, which tells us that Mary kept God's truth in her heart and meditated upon it. For Newman, Mary was a model of the true Christian and the Church. Within the heart of the Church, as it were, there is a meditation upon the truths of God revealed in Scripture and so within the life of the Church there is an advance in doctrine. To put it another way, within the prophetic tradition of the Church, its life and witness, the episcopal tradition of sound doctrine is enlarged as the Church meditates upon the mysteries of salvation.

Despite the signs that Newman's view of doctrinal tradition was becoming more fluid, he remained a critic of the Church of Rome. He believed that this Church had actually corrupted doctrine by adding to the orthodox exposition of the Faith of the Church produced by the Fathers in the period of the Councils of Nicea and Chalcedon. However, between 1839 and 1845 a number of factors—personal, temperamental, historical, and doctrinal—combined to bring about a gradual shift in Newman's ecclesiological viewpoint. The outcome of this slow change in perspective was the intuitive, imaginative conviction that the Roman Catholic Church was the answer to the simple question, "Where, what is this thing in this age, which in the first age (first few centuries) was the Catholic Church?" Yet his charge of corruption remained and before he could bring himself to follow his intuition and conscience and join the Church of Rome he had to deal with the obstinate difficulty of the charge. The result of this historical inquiry, the intensity of which his extant notebooks illustrate, was the *Essay on the Develop-*

9. *Fifteen Sermons Preached Before the University of Oxford* (1843), pp. 320ff.

ment of Christian Doctrine, which was written by September 1845 and published in November of that year. (This first edition was reprinted in 1974 by Penguin books and I shall quote from this edition.)

The Theme and Contents of the Essay

It is perhaps necessary, first of all, to give some attention to Newman's intuitive conviction concerning the primitive Church and the Roman Catholic Church. From 1839 to 1844 he gradually came to see that the complex reality of the Roman Catholic Church as he envisaged it corresponded more closely than any other claimant to the concrete reality of the Church of the Fathers. As he stated:

> Did St. Athanasius or St. Ambrose come suddenly to life, it cannot be doubted what communion they would mistake for their own. All surely will agree that these Fathers, with whatever differences of opinion, whatever protests, if we will, would find themselves more at home with such men as St. Bernard or St. Ignatius Loyola, or with the lonely priest in his lodgings, or the holy sisterhood of mercy, or the unlettered crowd before the altar, than with the rulers or the members of any other religious community. (p. 185)

Implied in this quotation are two convictions of Newman which he took for granted. First, he held, and had held as an Anglican, the view that the Church of the Fathers of the fourth and fifth centuries was the true successor of the Church of the apostles. He had leveled no serious charges of corruption against the Church of this period. Secondly, he took it for granted that if there is a revelation from God, then there must be but one revelation; further, since God rules the world providentially and since he desires that this revelation be always available to the world, then somewhere in the world there must be an authentic, adequate, and authoritative embodiment and expression of that revelation. Thus, Newman's choice was between the Roman Catholic Church and the Protestant denominations or National Churches (he never seriously considered the Greek Church), and he intuitively felt that his choice must be Rome.

Intuition was one thing, historical proof another. The historical difficulty Newman confronted was his charge that the Roman Church had corrupted doctrine. Previously, he had shared the common Protestant belief that during the Middle Ages (the "dark ages") there had been additions to and corruption of patristic doctrine. Stated another way, his problem was the lack of obvious resemblance between the Church of the apostles and of Athanasius, and the Church of Pope Gregory XVI (d. 1846).

Very much aware of this problem, Newman sought to provide, for his own personal satisfaction, a hypothesis to account for the difficulty. The hypothesis or theory was as follows:

> . . . that the increase and expansion of the Christian creed and ritual, and the variations which have attended the process in the case of individual writers and churches, are the necessary attendants on any philosophy or polity which takes possession of the intellect and heart and has had any wide or extended dominion; that, from the nature of the human mind, time is necessary for the full comprehension and perfection of great ideas; and that the highest and most wonderful truths, though communicated to the world once for all by inspired teachers, could not be comprehended all at once by the recipients, but, as received and transmitted by minds not inspired and through media which were human, have required only the longer time and deeper thought for their full elucidation. This may be called the *Theory of Developments.* (p. 90)

Basic to Newman's thought are two analogies, each of which merges easily and imperceptibly into the other. The first is that divine revelation is an *idea* which impressed itself upon the corporate mind of the Body of Christ. The second is that the growth of understanding of the meaning of revelation within the Body of Christ may be likened to the growth of understanding in the mind of the Christian believer.

Since the term "idea" is of great importance to Newman we need at this stage to be clear as to its primary meaning. It is, of course, closely related to the limiting model which he inherited from Locke and Hume; that is, an idea in the mind is formed from an impression of an external object. Yet Newman goes beyond the model and seems to ascribe to the idea:

> ... an organizing power and a fertility. ... The idea, far from being a mere copy or shadow and necessarily more ghostly than the reality to which it is related, turns out to be regulative, in that it excludes false developments of its inner content, and is continuously illuminating, in that it has a kind of inner dynamism which enables it to unfold more and more of its riches to that community of minds within which it dwells.[10]

To illustrate the first analogy of Newman—that divine revelation is an *idea* which impressed itself on the corporate mind of the church—I follow Owen Chadwick in using a modern analogy.[11] A young intellectual may have a general idea which influences his life; for example, "Social democracy is the best form of government for a country." This idea is at first vague, although it affects the political evaluations he makes and the journals and daily papers he reads. Only as this general idea is brought into contact with particular problems does he work out the theoretical and practical meaning of the idea. Thus, having this idea may mean that he finds himself obliged to oppose trading with countries ruled by dictators and obliged to support some kind of welfare system to help the needy and poor at home. In concrete situations and changing circumstances he works out his idea. The ramifications are implicit in the idea but not implicit in a logical sense. So, for Newman, Christianity is an idea, given to the world in Christ and by the apostles. What his idea means becomes obvious as the Church meets the heretic, engages in controversy, enters new cultures, faces social change, and seeks to evangelize. In these situations the Church sees new meaning in the idea and so defines this new meaning. Thus doctrine, tradition, and liturgy grow: "To live is to change, and to be perfect is to have changed often."

The second analogy is only minimally present in the *Essay* but it was used by Newman to explain to Roman Catholic theologians what he originally intended after they had misunderstood his argument. Just as the true convert to

10. J. M. Cameron, "Introduction" to Newman, *Essay* (Harmondsworth: Penguin, 1974), p. 40.
11. Owen Chadwick, *From Bousset to Newman. The Idea of Doctrinal Development* (London: Cambridge Univ. Press, 1957), p. 150.

Christ grows in a faithful understanding of Christianity, which at first he only appreciates in broad and probably vague outline, so also the Church grows in a slow understanding of Christianity. The love of the child for his mother is greater than any words he can use to express it, and so also is the relationship with God in Christ by the Holy Spirit which the Church enjoys. As Mary "kept all these sayings [of the angel from God] and pondered them in her heart"— so does the theologian and the Church.

In section three of the first chapter Newman sought to distinguish between the development and corruption of an idea and to assist in this task he made use of seven "tests of true development":

1. The preservation of the idea or type The essence of a philosophical or political system must be preserved as it meets changing circumstances or it can be said that corruption has occurred. For example, if the members of a monastic institution abandon their vows then the institution has not preserved the type.

2. The continuity of principles The basic principles of a country or movement must be preserved as it meets changing circumstances or it can be said that corruption has occurred. For example, when "we talk of the spirit of a people being lost, we do not mean that this or that act has been committed, or measure carried, but that certain lines of thought or conduct by which it has grown great are abandoned" (p. 126).

3. The power of assimilation In the physical world to grow is to live and it means taking in air and food. This assimilation is not always natural, for it may take effort. Yet, when a plant or animal ceases to assimilate into its body that which makes it live, it dies. Likewise any system of thought shows itself alive and grows as it assimilates into itself new material.

4. Early anticipation Though vague and isolated, anticipations of later large developments occur in the histories of nations and movements. For example, in the very early history of monasticism which had as an essential feature manual labor, there are indications that monks will in the future spend their times in literary pursuits. And, fulfilling this anticipation, much academic scholarship has come from monastic communities in modern times—such as the Benedictines of Paris who edited the works of the Fathers.

5. *Logical sequence* Newman did not mean a conscious reasoning from premises to a conclusion but that the faithful unfolding of an idea will produce developments which upon examination are logically related to the initial idea.

6. *Preservative additions*

> A true development may be described as one which is conservative of the course of development which went before it, which is that development and something besides: it is an addition which illustrates, not obscures, corroborates, not corrects, the body of thought from which it proceeds; and this is its characteristic as contrasted with a corruption. (p. 142)

7. *Chronic (of long duration) continuance* Corruption is distinguished from decay by its energetic action and it is distinguished from a development by its transitory character. Heresies, for example, are vibrant but do not last long whereas true developments continue through all difficulties.

Chapter two is entitled, "On the development of Christian ideas, antecedently considered" and takes up two themes: the probability of developments in Christianity and the probability of a developing authority in Christianity. The first theme has already been noticed in the discussion of his analogies. The second theme is very simple; it is that if there is a development of doctrine in the Church through history it is reasonable to suppose that God has provided a means by which the whole Church discerns *true* developments. For Newman, writes N. Lash:

> ... an argument from antecedent probability is not the imposition of a preconceived theory upon the evidence, but a more or less well-founded claim that it is reasonable to expect that, in a particular case, the data bear witness to one state of affairs rather than another.[12]

So, as part of the hypothesis of the development of doctrine, Newman included the hypothesis of the infallible authority

12. N. Lash, *Change in Focus* (London: Sheed & Ward, 1973), p. 90.

of the Pope of Rome to declare what were faithful explications of the idea of Christianity.

The remaining five chapters include a mass of historical information and interpretation. Aspects of the theological and liturgical development of Christianity in the Latin Church are subjected to the seven tests supplied in the first chapter. Thus, Newman was able to see the same doctrines (in their most attractive form), which the Reformers and many of Newman's former Anglican colleagues had regarded as corruptions, as developments of the original idea of Christianity. For example, the sacrament of penance was a development of the sacrament of baptism, and the cult of Mary was a development through the *theotokos* doctrine, or in other words, from the deity of Christ. To be as fair as possible to Newman it can be said that:

> ... what the arguments of his various "tests" do is to exhibit the "idea" of Catholic Christianity under various aspects and in connection with a great deal of historical data until, given it is a thing agreed upon that there is a Church dating from the time of the apostles and having a continuous historical existence, we are moved to affirm that the Roman Church of the year 1845 is the legitimate historical development of the Church, its development being such as we would expect or at least find not incredible.[13]

Newman offered the novel hypothesis of the *fact* of development and thereby affirmed that the common Roman Catholic hypothesis of the immutability of doctrine and the traditional Protestant hypothesis of the corruption of doctrine were unacceptable to him. He did not think that his *Essay* supplied a scientific proof or that he had provided a systematic, homogeneous theory of development. Rather, having come to the conclusion that Roman Catholicism embodied the one, true revelation, he believed he had supplied a persuasive apology, through the view of history he provided, for this conclusion.

Owen Chadwick has written that according to Newman, "the original revelation is unique: it was given partly in explicit doctrine, partly in feelings which were left to be

13. Cameron, "Introduction" to *Essay*, p. 47.

subsequently drawn out into doctrines."[14] This claim has been rightly questioned by other students of Newman. For example, Jan Walgrave writes that for Newman:

> All that the Church now believes or ever will believe is contained in the inspired records of what happened in Christ. Nevertheless, although entirely contained in the primitive Creed, the content of revelation is not explicitly unfolded in it. Through illuminating grace, revelation, presented to man by the words of the message, impresses on the mind of the faithful and the Church a real idea of the whole, imperfectly represented yet completely indicated by the scriptural message: "One thing only has to be impressed on us by Scripture, the catholic idea and in it they (the dogmas) are all included." Development, therefore, is not only the expansion in the mind of a wordless "idea-impression" but at the same time and in the same measure the explication of the content of the original message. That idea-impression is the living medium through which reflection unfolds the content of the message in a way that is faithful to its concrete fullness. It may be said, then, that the same process of development considered as a whole is as well a clarification of a presence of that whole to realizing apprehension as it is an elaboration of what is contained in the primitive message.[15]

And, as Nicholas Lash points out, "one of the devices which Newman employs to make good the claim that later doctrines are the explicit appropriations of 'aspects' of the one 'idea' is an analogy between the fulfilment of prophecy and the development of doctrine."[16] Newman adds:

> Thus too we deal with Scripture when we have to interpret the prophetical text and the types of the Old Testament. The event which is the development is also the interpretation of the prediction; it provides a fulfilment by imposing a meaning.[17]

The fact that Chadwick seems to have misunderstood Newman's exposition at this point illustrates how other men in the middle of this nineteenth-century controversy also misunderstood Newman's thought. Even today the careful reader of the *Essay* is left with a series of nagging questions,

14. Chadwick, *Bousset to Newman,* p. 157.
15. J. Walgrave, *Unfolding Revelation* (Philadelphia: Westminster, 1971), pp. 306–307.
16. Lash, *Change in Focus,* p. 93.
17. Newman, *Essay,* p. 155.

even though he or she may have a good knowledge of the rest of Newman's writings. This said, one cannot deny the force of the words of J. M. Cameron:

> There are certain works in the history of theology of which we can say that after their appearance nothing was ever again quite the same. We can say this of Augustine's *De civitate Dei*, of the *Summa theologiae* of Aquinas, of Calvin's *Institutes*. The *Essay on Development* is a work of this order and the first work by an Englishman—at least since the day of William of Ockham—to shake the theological schools of Europe. . . . The man whose genius has hitherto been given to the leadership of a counter-revolution in a National Church . . . is now become a power in Europe and the world.[18]

Roman Catholic theology was not prepared for Newman's original thinking in 1845. Even the broad-minded Italian, G. Perrone, to whom Newman sent a summary of his views in elegant Latin, could not truly appreciate it.[19] Neo-scholasticism, on the defensive in the mid-nineteenth century, could not come to terms with the idea of development and so it was not until the twentieth century that the work of Newman found wide acceptance within Roman Catholic thinking. Naturally, Newman was deeply disappointed that his hypothesis did not more widely commend itself to his new theological colleagues. However, he republished it in a new edition in 1878.

The Parallel Contribution of Johann Sebastian Drey and Johann Adam Möhler

It is now generally agreed that Newman produced his own theory of development quite independently of the views of development being taught at about the same time within the Catholic Faculty of Theology at Tübingen in Germany.[20] Drey made use of the idealistic philosophy of his day in order to emphasize the dynamic power of the Spirit in the community of the Church. On the basis of this approach he claimed

18. Cameron, "Introduction" to *Essay*, p. 7.
19. This summary was printed in *Gregorianum*, vol. 16 (1935), pp. 402ff.
20. For the Tübingen School see Mark Schoof, *Breakthrough: Beginnings of the New Catholic Theology* (Dublin: Gill & Macmillan, 1970), pp. 165ff.

that the doctrine of the Church is unchangeable in its essence, but adapts itself in its outward form to the needs of successive generations. Development, for him, was a sign of vitality in the Church, not a sign of departure from that which had always and everywhere been believed. The view of development expounded by Möhler in his *Unity in the Church from the Mind of the Early Fathers* (1825) continued with the insights of Drey. This book was actually the first infusion of patristic thought into the Catholicism of the Romantic period and was stimulated by the work of J. A. W. Neander, the Protestant historian. For Möhler, the Spirit arouses within the Church a common, shared consciousness of faith which both sustains and is sustained by God's revelation through history. On the basis of the inward principle of life, the Spirit calls the visible body of the Church into being. Thus, the mystical Church is rediscovered behind the structures of the juridical Church. Then these outward forms keep the inward tradition alive and allow it to grow. This whole process, though led by the Spirit, takes place at the level of outward forms in a kind of dialectical movement in which all kinds of realities such as heresies act as antitheses. Within this process the faith of the Church is extended.

If this seems to be a vague description of development, the fault is not wholly mine. Both Drey and Möhler expound the theme of progress in doctrine, but more vaguely than Newman. In later life Möhler modified his position in order to bring it nearer to that of his "orthodox" colleagues. Only in recent decades has the theology of the Tübingen school, like the teaching of Newman, made an impact on the thinking of Roman Catholic theologians as they wrestle with the problem of development of dogma.

CHAPTER TWO

THREE PROTESTANT RESPONSES

THE PUBLICATION of Newman's *Essay* was noticed by virtually every British theological and religious journal.[1] American and Continental publications also showed more than a passing interest in it. Reviews, nearly all critical, came from Anglicans, Baptists, Congregationalists, Presbyterians, Unitarians, and Roman Catholics. After a long examination the reviewer in the *Baptist Magazine* for 1846 concluded by saying: "We cannot but deplore the mischievous power of the system which he has embraced, to bewilder and enthrall a mind so highly gifted and so richly furnished" (p. 231). In this chapter I shall describe the reactions of three leading theologians. In choosing three I recognize my selectivity, but they are essentially representative of English, Irish, and Scottish Protestantism.

James Bowling Mozley (1813–1878)

Mozley, the son of a bookseller, studied at Oriel College, Oxford, where his brother Thomas was a Fellow. Here he became friendly with the leaders of the Tractarian Movement, particularly Pusey and Newman. About 1845 he be-

---

1. For a description of some of these reviews see David Nicholls, "Newman's Anglican Critics," *Anglican Theological Review*, vol. xlvii (1965), pp. 377ff.; and C. G. Brown, "Newman's Minor Critics," *Downside Review*, vol. lxxxix (1971), pp. 13ff.

came the editor of the *Christian Remembrancer,* a high-church magazine favorable to the Tractarian principles but critical of Roman Catholicism. Between 1850 and 1855 he modified some of his high-church views and ceased to be a supporter of the Oxford (Tractarian) Movement. Then he published several books for which he is well known: *On the Augustinian Doctrine of Predestination* (1855), *On the Primitive Doctrine of Baptismal Regeneration* (1856), and *A Review of the Baptismal Controversy* (1862).

His review of Newman's *Essay,* comprising some 65,000 words, was first published in the *Christian Remembrancer* in 1847. Following the republication of Newman's revised *Essay,* this long review appeared without changes as a book entitled *The Theory of Development* (1878). Mozley's review exhibits what Dean Church, the historian of the Oxford Movement, wrote of him: "After Mr. Newman, he was the most forcible and impressive of the Oxford writers," and he had "a mind of great and rare power, though only recognized for what he was much later in life."[2]

Since several of his friends had already published reviews, Mozley confined the scope of his review to what he called the argumentative part of the *Essay* rather than the historical.[3] In effect this meant looking at two major points—the definition of "development" and the crucial position claimed for the Bishop of Rome in the formation of doctrine.

Mozley agreed with his contemporaries that a "law of development" appeared to operate in many areas of human experience.

> It meets us in nature and art, in trade and politics, in life, vegetable, animal, intellectual. The seed grows into the plant, the child into the man; the worm into the butterfly, the blossom into the fruit. Education develops the individual, civilisation the nation. . . . (p. 3)

2. R. W. Church, *The Oxford Movement* (Chicago: Univ. of Chicago Press, 1970). Reprint of 1891 edition, pp. 203 and 318.
3. See further Andrew Mead, "Tractarian Criticism of Newman's Theory of Development" (B. Litt. thesis, University of Oxford, 1973) and P. Toon, *Evangelical Theology, 1833–1856* (London: Marshall, Morgan and Scott, 1978), chapter three.

Yet, if there was a law of development there was also a law of corruption. Mozley briefly explained this phenomenon.

> Legislators, philosophers, and founders of institutions are haunted by an image of a progress destined for their creations, which they never designed for them; and portend some departure from original principles which would elicit their protest, by anticipation, could they foresee it accurately enough. That things are better at first, and then deteriorate; that freshness and purity wear off; that deflections arise and that the inclination from the strict line, once made, widens with insensible but fatal steadiness; in a word, the tendency of things to degeneracy is one of those observed points which has naturalised itself in men's minds, and taken the position of an axiom. (p. 5)

This view of corruption sees it as being a departure from the original type. A contemporary example would be a government department, which in theory is intended to serve all the people justly, but in reality operates only for those who can pay a bribe or have a friend working there.

But, claimed Mozley, there is a further type of corruption. This is a corruption of exaggeration and excess in which the original type remains.

> Our final moral qualities are proverbially subject to this change. Courage becomes rashness, love becomes fondness, liberality becomes profuseness, and self-respect becomes pride. In these and such like cases the original type of virtue remains, but undergoes disproportion and disfigurement: the original disposition, which was good, does not evanesce and cease to be; but, continuing, is carried out beyond a certain limit, and transgresses some just standard. (pp. 6–7)

Again we may benefit from an example from the contemporary scene. Apartheid may be said to preserve the differences in the human race of which God is the Creator. Yet it preserves them in such an exaggerated way that equal respect and honor are not found in the system; instead, some are given excessive honor and others excessive shame.

Thus, in viewing the history of the expansion of the Church and of doctrine it is possible to interpret it with one or more of three models. There is the model of healthy development, the model of corruption, and the model of exaggerated or excessive development. Mozley pointed out that the charge made against Roman Catholicism by Anglican apologists had usually been that of corruption through exaggeration:

> The care for the dead, the veneration of saints, the peculiar reverence to the Mother of God, the acknowledgment of the change in the Eucharist, the sense of punishment due to sin, are all Christian feelings and doctrines, and they all exist in the Roman system; but they are asserted to exist in an immoderate and disproportionate way. The system which intensifies the spiritual by denying the material substance in the Eucharist [i.e., by transubstantiation]; which gives the Mother of our Lord, because great honour is due to her, the place which it does give her; which makes, because it was natural to imagine some purification of the soul before its entrance into heaven, the whole intermediate state a simple penal, fiery purgatory; which pushes out doctrines and expands feeling towards particular objects to the extent to which it does, has had one general fault very prominently charged to it, viz., that of exaggeration, including in that term all that, commonly called, extravagance, all that abuse and perversion of the exaggerative kind, which it practically means. (pp. 30–31)

This way of interpreting the Roman system as it existed in the nineteenth century was common to most orthodox Anglicans. As we shall see, some evangelicals tended to make more use of the model of corruption.

What orthodox Anglicans saw as exaggeration and excess Newman proclaimed as healthy development. Mozley concluded that Newman did not allow in his definitions of development and corruption the possibility of corruption through excess and exaggeration. For him, as long as the original type was maintained, there was no such thing as over-development, or excessive development. Marxism and democratic socialism can illustrate this point. Is Marxism a corruption in the sense of losing the original insights and principles of socialism, or is it only an excessive or exaggerated development of socialism? On Mozley's definitions Marxism can be a corruption either by losing the essential principles of democratic socialism or by over-developing those principles. On Newman's definitions it can only be a corruption by losing the essential principles.

Addressing himself to Newman's seven tests, Mozley claimed that they were unable to achieve their purpose as tests because the fact of development by excess was not allowed for by them; thus, they could not discover the corruption of exaggeration. In fact, Newman escaped this particular problem because he never saw or admitted that there was a problem. However, Mozley took one of the tests, that of "logical sequence," for he readily admitted that that which is logically derived from an acknowledged truth is as true as that from which it has been derived. To this test he brought Newman's use of the doctrine of the person of Christ and of purgatory as well as the cultus of the Virgin Mary. His reasoning concerning whether or not the development of the doctrine of Mary as *theotokos* into Mariology could be classed as logical is too involved to summarize here, and so perhaps is the Christology. However, what he says about purgatory is more easily summarized. The existence of purgatory, claimed Newman, is a corollary from the doctrine of repentance, for the former is contained in the latter. Necessary reasoning leads from the doctrine of repentance to the fact of purgatory, even though the Bible has no information on the latter. Mozley's rejoinder was that necessary reasoning did not lead in this way because repentance was a principle of the gospel while purgatory was a fact (a place/sphere between death and judgment for the endurance of pain for sin), and a general principle could not involve, logically, a fact. This point may be illustrated from the principle of charity—loving others as we love ourselves. If charity abides in my heart I am likely to help someone whom I judge is in need if I meet him or her at a particular place and time. But my action does not logically follow from the general principle of charity, for the action I take, though well meant, may in the long term be harmful or mistaken (through ignorance).

I now turn to the second major topic, of which Mozley wrote: "The doctrine of the Papal infallibility comes out as the keystone of Mr. Newman's whole argument, and according as he proves, or fails to prove, that doctrine, that argument stands or fails" (p. 83). Reduced to bare essentials, Newman's argument for the special place of the Bishop of Rome was, as Mozley saw it, the following: "That because God guarantees some truth, he must necessarily guarantee more: that because there is certainty to some extent, there must be certainty to a greater: that because an original act of revelation took place, it must be continued" (p. 93). This, agreed Mozley, was an attractive argument—but it was nothing more than a hypothesis, because no argument was supplied to place it beyond dispute.

At this point Mozley felt it necessary to examine Newman's claim that Bishop Butler, the expert on the doctrine of analogy and esteemed author of the *Analogy of Religion,* supported Newman's hypothesis. The result of the examination was as follows:

> On the whole, then, we say—according to the argument from analogy—an original creed or revelation thrown into the world of human intelligence is exposed to all common chances of human discolour in the carrying out; the substantial, original creed remaining throughout notwithstanding, and secured, if there be evidence for this fact, against failure to the end. And however, in reasoning *a priori,* out of our own heads, respecting revelation, we might expect it to do more for us because it did much, and look forward to a progress of truth pure, divinely guaranteed against error; the argument of analogy on the other hand bids us expect no such thing, but take the facts as they stand. It tells us not to expect all must be truth because there is truth; or again, to think all must be error because there is error; but to expect both truth and error. It supplies a dogmatic basis on the one side, and it allows for uncertainty on the other; and bids us neither be unbelievers nor perfectionists. It says—This is a mixed world and expect mixtures in it. (pp. 124–25)

Newman's hypothesis of papal infallibility could not be sustained by the use of analogy from nature, history, philosophy, or any other sphere.

Next, Mozley turned his attention to a further line or argument in the *Essay* which he saw as a *reductio ad absurdum.* This particular line of arguing instanced the Nicene Creed which Christians believe is essential and a development. Then it claimed that to accept the Nicene Creed is to accept the developmental principle, by which also must be accepted the whole cycle of Roman doctrine, including papal infallibility.

In challenging this argument, Mozley had to look initially at two possible definitions of the word "development." One definition is merely explanation: "A man in conversation makes an assertion, which another misapprehends; in reply he explains the meaning, or develops the meaning of his assertion" (p. 144). Cases of legal amplification illustrate the same principle. In ordinary language what a testator wants to say can often be said in a few sentences, but lawyers, having to guard against misunderstanding, expand or develop the ordinary language of the testator.

Another definition of development is the positive increase in the substance of a thing developed, a fresh formation not contained in, though growing out of, some original matter: "The development of a seed into a plant is one growth, for example; and it does not carry with it identity" (p. 146). In some cases, Mozley admitted, as in the development of a philosophical system such as Platonism, both definitions of development are used. There is development by explanation and by content.

This raised the question of the kind of development inherent in Nicene theology. Obviously, claimed Mozley, it was at least explanatory development, for it attempted to explain in Greek terminology *(homoousios,* etc.) the doctrine found in the New Testament that Jesus Christ is truly the unique Son of God. But was the Nicene theology a development by expansion also? Was there doctrine in the creed which is not found in the Bible except in a seminal form? Newman's whole argument was based on the fact that Nicene theology was more than explanatory development; it was a development by expansion, just as was the doctrine of purgatory or of Mariology. In reply, Mozley followed the arguments of the great Bishop Bull (whom Newman had followed prior to 1845) and appealed to the claim of the Nicene theologians and bishops that they were not teaching new or additional doctrine but only explaining what had been passed on to them. He wrote:

> We have the unanimous testimony of the whole body of Nicene fathers to the fact that they had received the doctrine they asserted from their predecessors in the Church; which predecessors had asserted that they had received it from their predecessors, and so on up to the age of the apostles. It was the full historical belief of the Nicene Church that its doctrine had been the doctrine of the ante-Nicene Church up to the commencement of Christianity. (p. 190)

Nicene theology might be a better explanation than the efforts of earlier writers but, claimed Mozley, it was not a change in doctrine. Furthermore, if Nicene theology is a development by expansion of earlier teaching, and if the Nicene doctrine is that the Son of God is truly of one essence with the Father, then earlier doctrine, particularly apostolic doctrine, was less than this; and original revelation did not include the doctrine of the full deity of Christ. Knowing Newman, Mozley was quite sure that he did believe that the full deity of Jesus Christ is taught in the New Testament.

In closing his long review Mozley joined other reviewers in making certain obvious observations. He remarked that Newman's presentation of expanding development was only a hypothesis and as such it was an entirely different hypothesis to that supplied by Roman Catholic theologians in their long controversy with Protestants. The traditional hypothesis denied development by expansion and only allowed for a development of explication, explanation, and logical deduction. For Mozley the new hypothesis was just as problematic as the old one. He could not see what was wrong with the traditional Anglican position which allowed a development through explanation, particularly in the doctrines formulated at the first four or five ecumenical councils. However, he was aware of the possibility of exaggerated development and deemed this to have occurred in medieval and Roman Catholic theology and practice. Newman's hypothesis, called a theory, was hardly a consistent theory:

> He professes a theory, but admits, as circumstances require, into it things which it does not account for. He has a theory on paper, and none in fact: he begins with philosophical simplicity and ends in arbitrary mixture. His theory is an inclusive one simply, and not an explanatory one; embracing a great

number of heterogeneous facts within one pale, but leaving them as far as ever from making one whole. We expected on opening this Essay to find Mr. Newman's theory for Roman facts, but we find nothing of the kind. What he does is to assert the old ultra-liberal theory of Christianity, and to join the Church of Rome; but he does not show—what it was the object of the Essay to show—the connection of the two,—the accordance of his theory with his act. And also professing to give us an hypothesis which accounts for and fits on to the facts of Ecclesiastical History, he ends with having an hypothesis indeed, and having facts, but having his hypothesis and his facts in separation. (pp. 225–26)

The "old ultra-liberal theory of Christianity," often called neology, was that view of the progress of Christianity taught by latitudinarians and deists in the seventeenth and eighteenth centuries, which gave little place to the authority of the Scriptures or ecumenical creeds.

William Cunningham (1805–1861)

William Cunningham became a minister in the Church of Scotland but at the Disruption in 1843 he was a leader of those who left the Kirk to form the Free Church. When New College, Edinburgh,was opened as the theological college of the new Church, he became a Professor and later the Principal. He was a learned man, primarily in orthodox Calvinism, and his outlook was little influenced by the winds of change which were blowing into Scotland from Germany. His major books were all published immediately after his death and they comprise collections of articles he wrote or lectures he delivered. These were *Discussions of Church Principles* (1863), *Historical Theology* (2 vols., 1862), and *The Reformers and the Theology of the Reformation* (1862).[4] The last two contain much material which illustrates Cunningham's view of the nature of doctrine and its development, but the material I primarily use here is taken from *Discussions* and originally appeared as a long article in the *North British Review* in 1846.[5]

4. The Banner of Truth Trust has reprinted *Historical Theology* and *The Reformers and the Theology of the Reformation.*
5. I use here material I wrote for the *Churchman,* vol. 89 (Jan. 1975).

Cunningham had followed the writings and careers of the Tractarians with some horror and was not very surprised when Newman joined the Church of Rome. He held that the *Essay* "might be justly regarded as being substantially an exposition of the process of thought by which he convinced himself of the truth of Romanism, and of the course of argumentation by which he thought that system could be defended" (p. 38). He was sure that the *Essay* did not detract from Newman's established literary reputation and that there was no ground for ascribing his conversion to Rome to any decay in his intellectual powers. However, Cunningham thought that:

> ... the work would probably have possessed a larger measure of personal interest if Mr. Newman had more formally set himself to describe the steps of his progress from the *via media,* which he formally occupied, to the extreme of Romanism—developing the changes which had taken place in his views from the commencement of the Tractarian movement till he found rest in an infallible Church, and the grounds on which he would defend them. (p. 39)

This point concerning the lack of a fully logical presentation of a case and the seeming confusion by Newman of the logical with the impressionistic is the basis for Cunningham's first criticism:

> Mr. Newman has an ingenious and subtle, but not a very logical mind, and he has taken no pains to explain the conditions and precise results of his argument, or to point out the exact way in which it stands related to and bears upon, the general argument between Protestants and Romanists. He does not indeed claim, formally and in words, for his theory, more than, if fairly supported, it is entitled to; but, by failing to mark out its true place and logical relations, and by introducing many collateral topics, he has succeeded to some extent, in conveying an impression, that he has achieved much more than, even if his theory were admitted, he could be fairly held to have accomplished. (p. 46)

To illustrate this criticism he then proceeded to examine what Newman said about Protestantism and Romanism.

Of Protestantism Newman had written: "Whatever be historical Christianity, it is not Protestantism...." Cunningham granted that this statement was true if by it is meant "that Protestantism has not always been the religion of Christendom, and that there was a period of above a thousand years when a religion materially different from it obtained, and to a large extent, in the professedly Christian Church" (p. 46). His point in reply was to state that the *proper inference from this accepted fact* is to ask the question, "What is the rule or standard by which we are to judge of what is or is not true or genuine Christianity?" Protestants, argued Cunningham, had no fear of either the historical investigation of Christianity or, more particularly, the investigation of Christian doctrines; for this study only revealed, in his opinion, the great difference between primitive Christianity and Romanism in the nineteenth century.

Turning to the claim that Romanism is historical Christianity, Cunningham first showed how Roman Catholic apologists had hitherto claimed an apostolic origin (either via the New Testament or unwritten apostolic tradition) for all their received doctrine and practice. Of such scholars he remarked that "they have never, indeed, attempted to adjust authoritatively the logical relations of tradition and infallibility; but they make tradition to establish infallibility, or infallibility to guarantee tradition, according to the exigencies of the occasion" (p. 49). Newman had seemingly changed the whole framework of the theological controversy between Protestants and Romanists by his theory of development which "cuts the knot but most certainly does not untie it" (p. 51). Cunningham continued:

> The theory of development, if established and conceded, merely removes a general preliminary objection against Romanism. It gives no positive weight or validity to any Romish arguments, but only clears the field for a fair discussion. It is but a substitute for the doctrine which the Romanists used to maintain—namely, that the apostles taught many things which were not contained in, or deducible from, the New Testament, but which might be learned from other sources; and as the old doctrine of tradition, or catholic consent required, in order to its serving any positive practical purpose in controversy, to be followed by specific proof of the apostolicity of particular tenets and practices, so the new

theory of development, even when proved or conceded, requires to be followed up by specific proof, that every Romish addition to the New Testament system is a true and legitimate development, and not a corruption. Mr. Newman does not formally deny that this is the true logical position and bearing of the theory of development, and indeed on several occasions he incidentally admits it; but he never gives to this idea anything like explicitness or prominence, and often writes as if he wished and expected it to be taken for something much more positive and effective. (p. 51)

Here, then, is the second example of the lack of logical precision in the *Essay*.

Turning his attention next to the actual theory, Cunningham found that "the following observations naturally suggest themselves":

First, it is wholly precluded—just as much so as the doctrine of tradition or catholic consent—by the proof of the perfection and sufficiency of the written word.

Secondly, it implies a virtual abandonment of the position hitherto generally occupied by Romanists in defending their cause, being a newly invented substitute for the ground on which all former defenders of Romanism—many of them men of great talent and ingenuity—had felt it to be necessary or expedient to take their stand. It is in the highest degree improbable, that a theory which was really sound in itself, and legitimately available for the defence of Romanism, should have been invented in the nineteenth century. Mr. Newman's statement that 'the view has at all times, *perhaps,* been implicitly (that is, without being explicitly stated) adopted by theologians', is unworthy of notice in an argumentative discussion. . . . De Maistre[6] and Möhler are the inventors of this theory of development and Mr. Newman himself is the first who has developed it. . . .

Thirdly, this theory of development is substantially infidel in its general character and tendency, and is evidently borrowed

6. Joseph De Maistre was a French Catholic writer whose writings provided the theoretical basis for the Ultra-montanist movement of the nineteenth century. He defended the infallibility of the Pope but saw that papal authority as having developed: "Everything that is lawful and is to exist for hundreds of years exists first as a seed and then develops." See further F. Heyer, *The Catholic Church from 1648 to 1870* (Naperville, IL: Allenson, 1969), pp. 132ff.

from German neology. No one who is acquainted with the writings of Popish controversialists will be in the least startled with this statement. They abound in infidelity and often contain elaborate expositions of the most plausible objections of scepticism. Their professed object in all this is, not to lead men to reject Christianity and revelation, but to shut them up to the submission to an infallible church. With this view they are accustomed to dwell largely upon the difficulties attending the proof of the truth of Christianity, and of the divine origin, canonical authority, genuineness, and integrity of the sacred Scriptures, the investigation of their true meaning, and the formation, from the study of them, of a definite system of faith and practice. (pp. 53–54)

Cunningham believed that, as an Anglican, Newman had sanctioned this kind of scepticism and that, having become a Romanist, it was not to be unexpected that he would propound an infidel theory—a theory which "manifestly implies that the revelation made by Christ and his apostles was very defective and imperfect . . ." and "that it stands much in need of enlargements and improvements . . ." (p. 55).

Being convinced that there was a definite relation between neology and Newman's theory, Cunningham referred to the *Institutiones Theologiae Christianae Dogmaticae* of J. A. L. Wegscheider (1771–1848), professor at Halle, which was first published in 1813, was in its eighth edition in 1844, and was usually reckoned to be the basic textbook of Neologian divinity. He wrote:

> The general position Wegscheider lays down is this: 'Religio Christiana ad majorem perfectionis gradum, evehi potest'; and, in explaining this position he makes an important distinction, which Mr. Newman has, we suspect intentionally, overlooked. 'Omnino autem in religionem major perfectio cadere dicitur, tam subjectiva quadam significatione, qua illius cognitio in hominibus perfectior reddi possit, quam objectiva, ita ut ea religionis doctrinae intelligatur indoles, quae permittit adeoque adjuvat et methodi et ipsius argumenti emendationem tempore procedente suscipiendam.' (p. 56)

A fair translation of the Latin for the first quotation would be "The Christian religion can be brought to a higher degree of perfection" and for the second quotation the following:

> All in all a religion is said to attain greater perfection both in
> what we might call a subjective sense, whereby men's knowl-
> edge of it can be made more perfect, and in an objective sense,
> which means that the nature of the religion's doctrines per-
> mits, and to that end promotes, improvement both of method
> and indeed content with the passage of time.

Wegscheider clearly made a distinction between subjective
development and objective development, claimed Cunningham, but Newman confused the two.

> He either does not see the important distinction, or he has
> carefully concealed it; and while it is perfectly manifest that
> an objective development alone can be of any practical use to
> him, he formally contends only for a subjective one, and brings
> to bear, as if in support of his theory, many analogies and
> illustrations, derived from the nature, operations, and
> progress of the human mind, the improvement of human
> knowledge, and other sources, which apply only to a subjec-
> tive, and not to an objective development. (p. 56)

Cunningham also believed that Newman manifested the
"same *ignoratio elenchi*" in his attempts to answer the objections to his theory: "The simple application of Wegscheider's
distinction shows at once that his answers to the objections
are utterly destitute of weight or plausibility, and leaves his
theory in all the nakedness and deformity of rationalism or
infidelity" (p. 57).

Other important criticisms made by Cunningham include the charge that Newman did not give any good reasons
for the abandonment of the old Protestant theory of the
gradual corruption of the Latin, Western Church (for which
see below) and the further charge that the use of the analogy
of the development of revelation within the Old Testament
period to illustrate the formation of Christian doctrines was
unacceptable. It failed, wrote Cunningham, in one essential
particular.

> . . . namely, that God made all these developments of previous
> revelations through inspired men, who were commissioned,
> not merely to develop previous revelations, but also to com-
> municate new ones. And as God has given us no inspired men
> since the time of the apostles, the fair inference is, that he did
> not intend to make any further objective developments of

previous revelations, which it would be incumbent on the Church to receive. (p. 64)

Cunningham's own view of the development of doctrine is basically a static one. Inside the Canon of Scripture, and more so in the Old than the New Testament, there is a development of doctrine within historical, inspired revelation. This "objective" development, guaranteed and controlled by God, does not extend beyond the apostles, with whom revelation ceases. Thus, only within the Canon of Scripture is God's truth to be found in its perfection and purity. Concerning the emergence of doctrines and dogma in the life of the Church, Cunningham had the following to say:

> There is a subjective development of Christian doctrine both in individuals and in churches, whereby men grow in the knowledge of God's revealed will and whereby theological science is extended and improved. But the result of this development is merely to enable individuals and churches to understand more fully and accurately, and to realise more thoroughly, *what is actually contained in, or deducible from, the statements of the written word, and can be shown to be so.* This, however, is essentially different from, nay, it is in a certain sense the reverse of, an objective development, which changes and enlarges or diminishes the external revelation, the standard or system of faith. (p. 56)

Therefore, he readily accepted an obvious subjective development in such documents as the Nicene Creed and the Westminster Confession of Faith.

However, accompanying the early subjective growth in understanding of such doctrines as the Holy Trinity and Christology, there was a growth of corruption in doctrine, organization, and worship. The latter Cunningham termed the:

> ... great Protestant position, that the Church gradually became corrupted in doctrines, government, and worship by departing from the scriptural and apostolic standard and that this is the true cause and explanation of the palpable contrast between the Church of the first century, and the Church at the beginning of the sixteenth century, or what is the same thing, the modern Church of Rome. (p. 60)

He went on to explain that the corruption which reached its height in the medieval Church had its origin in the agency of Satan and the depravity of man. Orientalism, Platonism, and polytheism were merely influences which at particular periods concurred with the basic abuses, but later modified their operations.

Naturally, Cunningham had a very high view of the Reformation: "We maintain that Protestantism was the Christianity of the apostles . . . and that the Protestantism (of the Reformation) was, to a large extent at least, a restoration of Christianity to its original, apostolic purity" (p. 47). And, as we shall notice shortly, he had a very high view of the Westminster Confession of Faith. At this point we can see that he has three interpretative models. There is the model of explanative (subjective) development by which Trinitarian and Reformational theology is understood; there is the model of corruption by which most of the medieval and Roman Catholic theology and practice is explained; and there is the model of restoration by which a claim is made that the Reformation churches contain the doctrine and life of the primitive Church.

As we turn briefly to notice how he related Calvin's theology to that of Theodore Beza and orthodox Calvinism we shall see that once more he had a model of explanative development in mind. The four points he discussed in chapter seven of *The Reformers and the Theology of the Reformation* (1862, reprinted 1967) were the eternal decrees of God, the imputation of Adam's sin to his posterity, the limitation of the Atonement to the elect, and justification through grace by faith. He recognized that on these points Calvin's teaching was not exactly the same as that of Beza and later Calvinists. There was a development of doctrine in the Calvinist tradition from Calvin through Beza and on into the Reformed tradition. As he could not believe that Beza had changed the emphases of Calvin, his explanation of the differences was on the basis of greater clarification after Calvin of that which Calvin taught. That is, had Calvin been alive to see what Beza and later "Calvinists" wrote, he would have agreed with them and acknowledged that they were only clarifying and stating more accurately what he had said. Whether or not Cunningham was right is a question which can be discussed, and we may judge that his rather simple explanation relative to subjective or explanative development is unsatisfactory. However, what we are noting here is the way in which he understood development.

William Archer Butler (1814–1848)

Brought up at his mother's wish as a Roman Catholic, Butler became an Anglican just before he entered Trinity College in Dublin. Here he displayed rhetorical, poetical, and philosophical gifts. In 1837, the year he was ordained presbyter, he became the first occupant of the chair of moral philosophy in Trinity College. It was in December 1845 that he produced his first "Letter on Mr. Newman's theory of development" for the *Irish Ecclesiastical Gazette,* a respectable, academic journal. This letter was followed by ten additional letters during 1846–47 which were later published as a volume in 1850 and in an improved edition in 1858 entitled *Lectures on Romanism.* Taken together, these letters form a learned criticism of the *Essay.* Unfortunately, they do not possess the readability and compactness of Mozley's criticism. The reason for this is that the author initially did not plan a critique of the *Essay;* rather, one letter led on to another and so on. This meant that subjects were repeated and there was no systematic argument. The material covers over 400 large pages.

To do justice to Butler's criticism of the *Essay* and to his own views on the development of doctrine would necessitate a *long* essay. Therefore, all I shall do here is to list the basic criticisms Butler made of Newman's presentation of the theory of development.

1. It is opposed to the received doctrine of the Church of Rome on Scripture and tradition.
2. It is a plain surrender of the traditional claims of Romanism to satisfactory evidence from antiquity.
3. It is actually condemned by the Tridentine Canons.

4. It makes unfair use of Butler's Analogy.
5. It uses the term "development" ambiguously.
6. It makes unfair use of the analogy of the development of doctrine within the prophetical revelation of the Old Testament.
7. It perverts the meaning of Christ's parables.
8. It substitutes historical eventuality for logical connection of disputed with admitted doctrine.
9. It misses the obvious point that true development would be a progress from simpler to sublimer things.
10. It makes history the law of doctrine.
11. It is impossible for it to set any limits to the future progression of doctrine.
12. It can be put to other uses than Newman used it—even to defend the Reformation and the Church of England.
13. It is inconsistent with the undeniable differences between the Eastern and Western Churches.
14. It is rationalism in Roman dress.
15. It does not teach that the apostles knew all *necessary* doctrine.
16. It confuses development with the work of systematizing and applying doctrine, which is the work of synods and doctors of theology.
17. The Roman primacy, so necessary for the guidance of development, did not arise until after the period when it would have been most necessary to safeguard development.

Despite these difficulties with development, Butler did ask: "Are there admissible developments of doctrine in Christianity?" His reply went as follows:

All varieties of real development, so far as this argument is concerned, may probably be reduced to two general heads, intellectual developments, and practical developments of Christian doctrine. By 'intellectual developments' I understand *logical inferences* (and that whether for belief or practical discipline) from doctrines, or from the comparison of doctrines; which, in virtue of the great dialectical maxim, must be true, if legitimately deduced from what is true. 'Practical developments' are the *living, actual, historical results* of those true doctrines (original/or inferential), when considered as influential on all the infinite varieties of human kind; the doctrines embodied in action; the doctrines modifying human nature in ways infinitely various, correspondently to the infinite variety of subjects on whom they operate, though ever strictly preserving, amid all their operations for effectually transforming and renewing mankind, their own unchanged identity. Intellectual Developments, it is thus obvious, are in the same sphere with the principles out of which they spring; they are (even when regarded with a view to rite and practice) unmingled doctrine still: *they are propositions.* Practical Developments, on the other hand, essentially consist of two very different, though connected, elements; divine doctrine, and human nature as affected by it; *they are historical events.* I am not aware of any thing reasonably to be called a development of Christian doctrine which is not reducible to either of these classes, the Logical or the Historical. (*Lectures,* pp. 57–58)

Thus, we see that his position was not very different from that of Cunningham. What to one was "subjective" development was to the other "intellectual" development. And for both, logical inference from revealed axioms in Scripture was important. The idea of practical developments is also found in other writers of this period who refer to the expansion of the Church in numbers and influence as development.[7]

7. For example, W. Gresley, *The Theory of Development Briefly Considered* (1846).

CHAPTER THREE

THE CONTRIBUTION OF ROBERT RAINY

REGARDED BY Prime Minister Gladstone as "unquestionably the greatest of living Scotsmen," Robert Rainy was Professor of Church History at New College, Edinburgh, for forty-four years and concurrently served as Principal for thirty-two years.[1] He studied under William Cunningham before his ordination into the Free Church of Scotland ministry, and after eleven years as a parish minister became a professor and later the leader of the Free Kirk.

In 1873, the year before he became Principal, he delivered the fifth series of Cunningham Lectures in Edinburgh under the title, *The Delivery and Development of Christian Doctrine,* and published them a year later. Ten years earlier he had written on Newman's theology in the *North British Review* and found that the theory of development would command his interest for a longer period.[2] Having traveled and studied in Germany, he was aware that those who were called "the believing theologians" (e.g., Isaac Dorner, author of the massive *History of the Doctrine of the Person of Christ,* E.T. 1861) were representing the history of the formation of

---

1. For the life of Rainy see P. C. Simpson, *Principal Rainy,* 2 vols. (Edinburgh, 1909).
2. See further Simpson, *Principal Rainy,* vol. 1, p. 289. The article appeared in October 1864.
3. Simpson, *Principal Rainy,* vol. 1, p. 181.

doctrine as a development. Further, he well knew that in Britain, though many were ready to admit the idea of development in Christian doctrine, this was done "with little regard to the ground on which it should be placed, or to the consequences which may be involved in it!"[3]

I am devoting a whole chapter primarily to the contribution of Rainy because his book is the only full-length, positive treatment of the subject of development to come from the pen of an evangelical in the nineteenth century. Further, it is a valuable contribution which is regrettably hardly known, even by evangelicals.

We shall see that a very different ethos pervades the writing of Rainy and his teacher, Cunningham. Rainy was not so learned in the controversial divinity of the sixteenth and seventeenth century, but he did read German and so could enter into a vast territory of historical and theological learning denied to Cunningham. In addition to their difference in reading matter, they differed in tenor of mind. Cunningham possessed a dogmatic and systematic mind which was more efficient and perhaps happier in dealing with logical deduction than in sifting complex historical evidence. Rainy possessed an orderly mind, open to new ideas, given to finding an honorable compromise, and happier discussing possible answers to problems than in asserting that there was only one definitive answer. Unlike Cunningham, who had fought for his convictions and beliefs in the events which led up to the Disruption in Scotland in 1843, Rainy had come to his own views in a more leisurely manner, including a period of study in Germany. Cunningham was the solid, scholastic High Calvinist of the early Victorian era while Rainy was the cultured, moderate Calvinist of the later Victorian era.

Development in Scripture

In the opening lecture, Rainy explained the ground over which he intended to travel. He pointed to the great and notorious disagreements among Christians concerning doctrine and confessions of faith and suggested that these pre-cipitated the answering of two questions: What are the conditions under which, and the limits within which, the human mind may be warranted in laying down doctrines? And, how far can we reasonably think that the Bible was designed to furnish us with materials to be used in this way—to be fused and reproduced in these definite and in-variable forms? He referred to the different approaches to the history and emergence of doctrine and dogma entertained by Roman Catholic and Protestant scholars, and here he noted the impact of Newman's theory. He briefly de-scribed the latitudinarian or neologian interpretation of Christianity and its history in which development is portrayed as reaching its climax in the rationalist and moralist view of religion entertained by recent British and German "unbelieving theologians" such as Lessing. He also demon-strated his awareness of the many Germanic studies of the history of doctrine. Finally, he announced his resolution that his study would cover four areas: the way in which doctrine is delivered in the Bible, the manner in which doctrine is a function of the believing mind, what is meant by the development of doctrine, and the place of creeds and confessions in the Church.

The second lecture is concerned with the delivery of doctrine in the Old Testament. He argued that God's teach-ing of men and revealing of his mind to men was progressive in history, was related to divine acts (e.g., the Exodus) and divine transactions (e.g., covenants) and, while having a definite relation to the present, pointed to the future, fuller revelation from God in the Messiah. He observed that there was a real identity of faith and fellowship with God where there were great differences of knowledge about God—as between the earliest and latest Old Testament believers—and that there was *"a much-more-ness"* in God's mind than in the minds of believers.

> This *much-more-ness* is asserted not of God's mind as it is in itself merely, but as it is embodied in his present words and acts. Neither the thoughts, nor the prayers, nor the faith, nor

> the thanksgiving of God's people, have ever borne any proportion to the height, and depth, and length, and breadth of his thoughts which were towards them. (p. 72)

Two further observations were that "the Old Testament system of dealing with the Church implies a fuller revelation of doctrine in reserve, awaiting the Church at some future stage" and that God spoke not merely to the intellect of men but rather to the whole man, demanding not only the agreement of the mind but also moral sympathy.

In the third lecture he turned to the delivery of doctrine in the New Testament. Here his study led him to emphasize two features. First of all, doctrine is not provided there relative to independent propositions or axioms but is rather related to events and people:

> The Christian doctrine rests upon and rises out of the Christian facts—the persons, the transactions, the events. These come before us in a purely historical way; and out of them, rising out of the history, comes the teaching: what we are to think of God, of man, of Christ; of what He came to do and did; of the principles of truth that are honoured, illustrated and made effectual by Him. So, also, all obligations and all hopes come before us as principles of truth flowing out of what man has shown himself to be, what God has done or is to do. (pp. 100–101)

Secondly, doctrine is addressed to, and is meant to affect, the whole person.

> It is characteristic of Christian doctrine that it is delivered to be the light and guide of Christian life. It is not meant for mere gratification of speculative curiosity, or for rounding off a system. As it radiates from history—a divine history—so it is meant to pass over into another history, our own. In a word, it comes to illuminate and guide the life of renewed men. This does not imply that we are to measure our faith in the truth by our perception of its bearing on practice. It may well be that it has various bearings on practice, even in our own case, which our analysis is unable to detect or to assign. (p. 102)

So he emphasized that "the truth is set forth in the Scripture not statically, but dynamically; not in mere abstract conception, but as the rule of spiritual forces and the *rationale* of spiritual events" (p. 104).

He was also conscious of what today is called the variety of theologies in the New Testament:

> There is a distribution of doctrine among the inspired servants of God, so that we find ourselves, in some respects, in a different region as we pass from the writings of one to the writings of another. Words, phrases, doctrines, seem to assume a new turn, and to stand in new relations. This is very intelligible, if we remember that the divine fulness of the truth bears on human beings in ways that are very various. It is not a diversity in the being of truth that here appears, but a diversity in the manner of its going. (p. 105)

And this divine diversity is a pregnant revelation ever fresh and adequate, able to guide the men of God at all stages of the history of the Church.

The Nature of Human Doctrine

From the delivery of doctrine in Scripture, Rainy turned to the believing and confessing of doctrine by the individual and the Church. This particular lecture is crucial for his whole presentation and exhibits the careful thinking he had done (and which Christians constantly need to do) concerning truth as it exists in God's eternal mind, as it is presented in the historical revelation recorded in the Bible, and as it is understood by Christians of different times and places. Many of us have a tendency to conflate these areas, but Rainy was right to distinguish them—particularly the last two categories—for the problem of the development of doctrine will never be understood by those who claim that they are exactly reproducing biblical teaching when they preach or create doctrine.

Doctrine, for Rainy, was a determination of what Christians believe to be true on the authority of the revelation they have patiently and prayerfully studied. He used the word "determination" as an indication that doctrine must have clarity and precision in order to distinguish it from a vague impression in the mind. Doctrine was produced by the intellect—the result of rational reflection. But the creation of doctrine obviously is not a necessary activity of the mind of all believers, for many believers do not have clear doctrinal formulations. Other believers have intellectual processes which are more developed. As these believers with active intellects read and study Scripture, they are not only inspired to love, worship, and serve God, but also inspired to seek an answer to the question—what is true? Now this question will take different forms according to the subject matter being prayerfully read—for example, what is true about God's character, what is the relation of Jesus to God the Father, and what is the connection between regeneration and conversion? In answering the question, "What is true?," the believer, be he a layman or professional theologian, creates a doctrine which is a fairly precise determination.

Rainy emphasized that in Scripture the divine teaching is implicated with an appropriate significance for feeling, life, and worship (e.g., the doctrine of predestination in Ephesians 1 where the teaching is related to worship and service). And, stated Rainy:

> In which more complete form I also probably should habitually present it if I were inspired, or if in me the unity of an enlightened understanding, and a sanctified heart, and a will at one with all goodness, were finally attained. But as it is, I have to make my way into it, by realising the separate elements of the case. I have to isolate and make sure of the exact fact, or relation, or principle to be believed for truth; and for the purpose of doing this, and presenting to myself what I seem to have learned on this side, I must select words which enable my mind to mark how it is taught to think, as well as how it is taught to feel or act. (pp. 114–15)

Thus, doctrine is the creation of the believing mind or intellect. "As held and uttered by the believer and by the Church, doctrine is formally human. It is the echo to the divine voice. It is the human response to the divine message. It is the human confession of the divine gift" (pp. 117–18). And he went on:

> The meaning of the Scripture teaching, as it delivers the doctrine that is according to godliness, is what God meant, what the inspired man meant, or the Spirit in which he spake. The meaning of the doctrine, as we confess it, is what we mean, what men mean, and what the Church means.

This distinction, however, implies no antagonism, for human doctrine attempts to state what God means in his revelation to us. Conscious that some men admitted a distinction only between truth in the eternal mind of God and truth in human credal statements, he emphasized that while he saw a distinction between the truth in God's mind and truth in divine revelation, he also saw this further distinction of divine teaching in revelation and human doctrinal formulations. This latter distinction he illustrated with reference to Jesus Christ:

> His words were human words, and indeed of the plainest; and the meaning they carried was such as existed in his mind in the form of human thought. However, it was human thought of such an order, and so related to eternal truth, and the words employed were chosen with so supreme dominion over the resources of expression, that the history of his Church has been all along a history of human minds entering into his mind, it remains that there is a contrast between the plenitude of his utterance and the measure of our insight. (pp. 123–24)

We enter into the mind of Christ but we do not fully think his thoughts.

The creation of doctrine by the Church, or a branch of it, is a collective enterprise performed for the whole society by those with special gifts and aptitudes. As the Church is neither perfect nor infallible, she embodies on a larger scale the relation of the believing mind to the inspired Scriptures. Here doctrine is therefore human doctrine and open at all times to improvement. It is this doctrine which is taught by her pastors and teachers and is thus passed on with the Scriptures from generation to generation.

In the second part of this fourth lecture, Rainy answered the objections of those (e.g., Matthew Arnold, *Literature and Dogma,* 1873) who taught that Scripture is not by its nature fitted to yield doctrinal conclusions that are valid and reliable. This exercise led him to comment on the use of inference in reaching theological conclusions—a topic always of interest in Calvinist circles. Here he was cautious and could not claim, as Cunningham had done, that what is deducible from the truths of Scripture is as sure as that from which it has been deduced. He admitted that there are some inferences so obvious as not to be questioned (e.g., if it is true that all men are sinners, then it follows that I am a sinner). However, according to Rainy, there are certain practical limits to the use of inference. First of all:

> ... the measure of truth depends on the ends which the Revealer had in view. That knowledge conferred on us, sufficient for its own end, is in no sense complete knowledge, and for any end but that intended is insufficient knowledge. The moment our reasoning goes beyond the *intended* scope designed for us by the Teacher, and indicated in the general drift of Scripture, it stumbles into all the dangers of ignorance. (p. 164)

An example of false reasoning would be the deduction that because there is one person (*hypostasis* and *prosōpon*) of the Lord Jesus there is in him only one nature or one will. Secondly:

> ... we reason by means of terms in which our doctrinal statements are expressed. Our confidence is, that those terms, as used by us, substantially express and interpret Scripture thoughts. ... But when we ... begin to reason *from* our doctrinal position the risk becomes the greater. The inference may be drawing its strength from that excess or defect in our thought, or our term, wherein it fails, and betrays to a higher mind its weak and fallible origin. (p. 165)

An example here would be to deduce from the doctrine of particular redemption (limited atonement) the doctrine that the gospel should not be preached to all, and all should not be urged to obey and believe the gospel. Therefore, he was only prepared to defend the use of inference in a carefully circumscribed way.

He concluded this long lecture by urging that we must always allow the Scriptures to inject life and meaning into our doctrinal formulations. His example was the doctrine of the Trinity which, when read in the cold terminology of its expression in the Athanasian Creed, appears to be far removed from the dynamic truth contained in Scripture. However, when it is read alongside Scripture, it can magnificently translate into careful and precise propositions that which is conveyed by the whole of Scripture.

Development in History

Having set the context by explaining how divine teaching appears in Scripture and how doctrine is formed in the believing mind, Rainy continued in the fifth lecture to explain how he understood the development of doctrine. He began by making reference to the theory of development both in rationalist theology and in Newman's *Essay*. Then he briefly explained the "old Protestant position" of an original purity of faith in the early Church, corrupted by Antichrist, and restored by the Reformers. As an example of this interpretation, set out on a grand scale, he referred to the books produced by the Magdeburg Centuriators, the *Historia Christi* (1559–1574), which claimed that the early Church began with pure "Lutheran" teaching which was corrupted by Satan in the Middle Ages and restored to its pristine condition by Luther.

Rainy also admitted that the Protestant opponents of Newman in 1845–47—and he instanced W. A. Butler—had denied any notion of development except the explanative or the logical type. Yet he observed that those who were most rigid in excluding development commonly were obliged to admit that inevitable processes were at work in the Church which often produced changes in the modes of statement and of explanation adopted. Also, the believing theologians in Germany had been making use of the model of development in their writing of history. Thus, he claimed that:

> The great rationalistic movement of the last century and of the present has produced, amid many evil consequences, this good one, that an appeal to facts and an investigation of them have been carried out with more resolute disregard of consequences than at any previous period. The results of modern historical research certainly exhibit a succession and growth in the history of doctrine which corroborate the belief, that development of some kind or other, explained by one principle or other, must be acknowledged. (p. 182)

Few historians today would quarrel with this statement, and so he now was able to state the object of this lecture. It was:

> . . . to assert and vindicate development of doctrine as a function of the Church of Christ, belonging to her duty, connected with a right use of her privileges, and indeed indispensable to her life. It is asserted as a source of change and advance, not sudden, impulsive, and fitful, but commonly slow, secular and cumulative. It is asserted as consisting well with all that Protestants hold of the completeness, perfection and clearness of the word of God, and therefore as free from implication with the principle of Rationalism on the one hand, and with the principle of Romanism upon the other—with both of which it has been represented as allied. It is asserted as necessitated *a priori* by the nature of the case, and proved in fact *a posteriori,* from the evidence of history. (p. 183)

Such an aim would have been incomprehensible to Cunningham, and the fact that Rainy asserts it so boldly reveals the powerful impact of the beginnings of modern historical research upon educated men.

Since he believed that confusion had arisen in many minds concerning the point from which development might be said to have begun, he attempted to clarify this point. If the starting point is the completed revelation given to the Church in the Scriptures, then difficulties arise. For example, how can the Scriptures be a complete and adequate rule of faith if they serve only as a point of departure for a development through history? Development:

> . . . starts from the measure of understanding which the Church had of the Revelation at the time when apostolic guidance ended; it starts from the measure of attainment in knowledge of the meaning, scope, and connection of the truth set forth in apostolic teaching and embodied with other elements in the Scriptures. (pp. 184–85)

Rainy held that the difference:

> . . . between the completed Revelation and the Church's apprehension of it, was as great as that between the brightness of the sun and the reflection of it in some imperfectly-polished surface, that gives it back again really, constantly, but with a diminished, imperfect, wavering lustre. (p. 185).

Since many have supposed and claimed that the generations immediately following that of the apostles must have had full and clear doctrinal understanding, Rainy attempted to show that this was unlikely. It was not his intention to depreciate the knowledge of the Christians of the second century as the school of F. C. Baur tended to do.[4] He did not doubt that these Christians probably had a highly developed spiritual and moral awareness and were well grounded in basic Christian facts; for example, that Christ died for our sins. Yet he rightly claimed that this type of knowledge did not necessarily include clear and precise doctrinal expressions on such matters as the nature of God and of Jesus Christ. Such precision in doctrine was not needed, for the questions to which later dogma and doctrine were the answers provided by the Church had not yet been raised. Thus, he was able to emphasize again that the possibility for the development of doctrine fitted well with the known condition of the early Church.

His next task was to indicate what were the historical factors or impulses which caused the Church to formulate doctrines. The first of these was "the collision of the Faith with the mass of impression and opinion pre-existing in the world" (p. 208). Here he had in mind the varieties of ancient philosophy and that strange mass of speculation which we call Gnosticism. All these systems in one way or another challenged the Christians to think out and state their own explanation for the universe and the people in it. Then, secondly, there were the heresies which arose within the Church to challenge the common understanding of the gospel within the Church. For example, Arianism in the fourth century taught that Jesus Christ was not God made man, and in reply the Church—led by the Emperor—stated very clearly in the Nicene Creed of 325 the precise relation of Jesus to God the Father. A third impulse, which only came into full flower in the Middle Ages, was the systematizing

4. For the school of Baur see P. C. Hodgson, *F. C. Baur on the Writing of Church History* (New York: Oxford Univ. Press, 1968) and *The Formation of Historical Theology: A Study of F. C. Baur* (New York: Harper & Row, 1966).

tendency—the effort to connect all doctrines together in a reasoned and adjusted system. The *Summa Theologica* of Thomas Aquinas is the most famous example of this tendency.

Rainy could have mentioned other impulses such as the influence of the liturgy and popular devotions upon doctrine, but he was surely right to emphasize the importance of the questions raised for the Church by enemies without and heretics within. He was also right to clarify that the formulation of doctrine by the Church over the long centuries from Ignatius of Antioch to Luther of Wittenberg was not a simple, smooth, or regular development. There were sound developments (e.g., the dogma of the Trinity) and there were false ones (e.g., the early heresy of Sabellianism and the medieval doctrine of transubstantiation). He held that the history of the church in this department of doctrine has not proceeded according to any theoretical or ideal program.

> It has included much that did not spring from her proper destiny or privilege; not only sound development, but unsound and erroneous divergence. Melancholy aberrations led her at last into a wilderness of errors, so as greatly to mar the fruit even of those sound attainments in doctrinal truth which were still retained. I say that those aberrations led *the Church;* for, as I have already remarked, whatever we may hold of a remnant preserved when general apostasy had fallen upon Christendom, we cannot doubt that the prevailing condition of things involved them also in great darkness and bewilderment. (p. 221)

Perhaps today we would want to give a more positive estimate of the religion of Christendom in the Middle Ages; but at the same time most would, like Rainy, have their suspicions about the existence of a pure remnant existing in Albigensian and Waldensian congregations in this period.[5]

Thus, Rainy leads us to the period of the Reformation:

> The Reformation was a great doctrinal development. It was not merely and only a clearing away of corruptions and superstitions, and a regress to some standard of early attainment. Nay, it was not only a regress to the Scriptures themselves; it

5. See J. Pennington, "The Waldensians as the Evangelical Pipeline," *Colloquium,* vol. 3 (1969), pp. 229–237. Albigensians were heretical.

was also a progress in the Scriptures. It involved a positive
hold on truth doctrinally, especially on some truths, such as
constituted a positive advance and progress in insight into the
Scriptures, as compared with anything that had been attained
before in the history of the Church. That this great providential blessing was not duly improved, that it was in various
ways mismanaged and marred by the generation on which it
fell, and others that came after, is but too like the common
history of God's best gifts. Nevertheless, the attainments of
the Reformation go down to all following generations, placing
them in a different position with reference to doctrinal knowledge from that occupied by any generation which went before.
(p. 222)

Cunningham's interpretative model for the Reformation
was that of restoration—the restoring of the primitive face
and doctrine of Christianity. Although Rainy preferred the
model of development and the expansion of doctrinal understanding in the Church, he was also too much the historian
not to recognize that with positive development there came
other false developments which served to divide the Church
and to hide the light which was beginning to shine clearly
from Scripture. (I regret that he did not comment on the
relationship of the Westminster Confession of Faith to that
of sixteenth-century Reformed or Protestant theology. These
comments would have given us a greater understanding of
how he viewed the development of doctrine since the Reformation.)

As a theologian Rainy believed:

. . . that the gracious presence and working of the Holy Spirit
does not forsake the Church. He so presides and influences, as
to secure that the whole course of things shall be a history of
grace dealing with men in a manner worthy of God's mercy
and patience. (p. 222)

However, he held that the way God guided and acted gra-
ciously was hidden from us. This belief in the secret providence of God linked to his doctrine of private judgment (the
right of the individual believer to judge for himself the
meaning of Scripture) led him to state the following: "It is a
vain thing to talk of fixing, by any internal test or criterion,
which are the legitimate and which are the spurious de-

velopments" (p. 223). In a later chapter I shall challenge this claim.

Yet Rainy believed there was an inner direction to all genuine development: "It is a development up to the Scriptures; and the Scriptures always are above it, as the perfect standard never fully reached" (p. 226). This assertion sounds attractive, particularly to those who wish to preserve the perfection and sufficiency of the Scripture and still maintain the need for doctrinal development. However, it is not entirely satisfactory because in Scripture, as Rainy himself conceded, truth appears in such a way as to fire the imagination, touch the heart, open the eyes, and impel the will of the Christian reader. In doctrinal formulations the senses, feelings, and will are being bypassed in order to appeal primarily to the mind or intellect. Thus, even the very best doctrinal formulation cannot ever be on the same level as the presentation of divine teaching in Scripture. Yet, he is right insofar as the existence of Scripture always causes the theologian to recognize the delicacy and humanity of the theology he creates and handles.

Creeds and Confessions

The final lecture is about creeds and confessions of faith in the Church. Rainy provided a charitable yet forceful argument in favor of confessions of faith as subordinate standards in churches, pointing to the final authority of Scripture. He believed the churches should utter their present faith so as to bring out the consent of past ages with their own; and he held that there is truth attained in the Church which abides from generation to generation, though he recognized that not all is truth which the Church of any age may be disposed to take for the truth. This being the case, he wrote:

> Therefore we are glad to recognise in the early creeds the hand of God leading the Church to modes of utterance which we can take up and affirm. We rejoice in the harmony of the Reformation confessions, and we feel no cause to be ashamed of the strength and symmetry of that which we receive. But with all

this, it must be affirmed unequivocally, that all these exist subject to correction. This concession must not be a mere idle flourish; it must exist in the Church as a living, practical, powerful principle. Loyalty to God's supreme word requires it; and where it is withdrawn or denied, the defence of creeds, on Protestant principles, becomes impossible. (pp. 273–74)

Thus, he advocated that the ministers and elders of his own denomination be prepared, as occasion demanded, to modify or change the Westminster Confession and Catechisms.

Here our summary of Rainy's book ends. In his *The Ancient Catholic Church* (A.D. 98–451), published in 1902, he gave further indications of his views on development. These occur in his final chapter entitled "Processes of Change." Apart from this he does not appear to have written anything further on the topic of development. What he did write remains valuable and should perhaps be read by those who, having obtained recent reprints of the works of William Cunningham, may be tempted to think that all major evangelical Presbyterians of the nineteenth century shared Cunningham's views on the formation and corruption of doctrine.

The Views of Charles Hodge (1797–1878)

Before closing this chapter it will be instructive to notice the views on development of Charles Hodge, whose famous *Systematic Theology* was in the final stages of publication when Rainy was delivering his lectures in Edinburgh. Hodge's views are stated briefly and succinctly in chapter five of his first volume. Referring to the information about German theology provided by Philip Schaff (1819–1893) in his *What is Church History?* and *Principles of Protestantism,* Hodge condemned the theory of development as used by German rationalist theologians. He did, however, state a positive view of development. With reference to the analogy of the scientific method of his time (to which he was very committed) he claimed:

All Protestants admit that there has been, in one sense, an uninterrupted development of theology in the Church, from the apostolic age to the present time. All the facts, truths, doctrines, and principles, which enter into Christian theology, are in the Bible. They are there as fully and as clearly at one time as another; at the beginning as they are now. No addition has been made to their number, and no new explanation has been afforded of their nature or relations. The same is true of the facts of nature. They are now what they have been from the beginning. They are, however, far better known, and more clearly understood now than they were a thousand years ago. (pp. 116–17)

So he argued that it was *natural* that there should be development of theological knowledge. In the Bible, God's truths "are not systematically stated, but scattered, so to speak, promiscuously over the sacred pages, just as the facts of science are scattered over the face of nature, or hidden in its depths" (p. 117). Therefore, it has taken many years for these facts to be collected, sifted, and stated. As in the history of science this process has included false theories. But there has been progress in understanding and thus development of doctrine has occurred.

Hodge proceeded to argue that what is natural and reasonable is also a historical fact. The Church has advanced in theological knowledge.

The difference between the confused and discordant representations of the early Fathers on all subjects connected with the doctrines of the Trinity and of the Person of Christ, and the clearness, precision and consistency of the views presented after ages of discussion, and the statement of these doctrines by the Councils of Chalcedon and Constantinople, is as great as between chaos and cosmos. And this ground has never been lost. (p. 118)

Also, the Augustinian teaching on sin and grace and the Reformation doctrines of the work of Christ and the application of salvation by the Holy Spirit had not been lost. We may add that Hodge believed that the Westminster Confession contained further development relative to the divine decrees, federal theology, and the theme of particularity in election, atonement, and salvation. As taught by his son Archibald, by B. B. Warfield, J. G. Machen, and others,

Charles Hodge's view of development has been influential in Calvinist circles, providing great confidence in the verity of "Westminster" theology.[6]

6. For Machen's views see J. H. Skilton, ed., *Scripture and Confession* (Nutley, NJ: Presbyterian & Reformed, 1973), pp. 150ff. Warfield's are noticed in the next chapter.

CHAPTER FOUR

THE CONTRIBUTION OF JAMES ORR

IN 1901, JAMES ORR of Glasgow published his *Progress of Dogma*. Not only did this book provide a theory of the development of doctrine, it also illustrated the theory with a description of the emergence of specific doctrines. It was an evangelical reply to the views on development of Newman and Adolf Harnack of Germany. Since we have examined Newman's theory it remains for us to look at Harnack's before we examine the views of Orr.

Adolf von Harnack (1851–1930)

Since 1886, no serious student of the history and development of dogma has been able to avoid studying the contribution of Adolf Harnack. In that year the first volume of his *History of Dogma* was published. An English translation of the third German edition first appeared in 1894 and the final German edition was published in 1909–1910. Jaroslav Pelikan has recently written:

> Harnack's *History of Dogma* is probably still the most influential account of the genesis and evolution of Christian doctrine. Although Harnack's version of one or another chapter in the history of doctrine has been superseded in the monographic literature, it is still to his overall account of historical theology that readers of all theological persuasions continue to turn.[1]

1. J. Pelikan, *Historical Theology* (Philadelphia: Westminster, 1971), p. 66.

Before describing Harnack's theory of the development of dogma it will be useful to explore his stature as a historian. Born in Dorpat, Esthonia, the son of a professor of practical theology, he quickly moved through the academic hierarchies—from Leipzig to Giessen, from Giessen to Marburg, and Marburg to Berlin. In Berlin, apart from the professorship of Church history, he was appointed director of the Royal Library. Honored by the Kaiser in 1914, he became Adolf *von* Harnack. The basic foundation for his work in the history of dogma rested in his study of early Christian literature. He excelled in textual study, his work on Marcion and the literature of the early Church still often consulted. It was his conviction that the center of gravity of Church history as a scholarly field rested in the Church history and the history of dogma of the first six centuries. He fervently believed that one important result of his work as a historian studying the "facts" was the discovery of the "reality" or the "essence" of Christianity. He sought to describe this reality in sixteen public lectures delivered in Berlin in 1899–1900. When published under the title, *Das Wesen des Christentums,* it became a best-seller. The English translation was entitled *What is Christianity?* States Pelikan:

> Although it has been customary for writers on Harnack to stress the theological presuppositions of the *History of Dogma* and to find these spelled out in *What is Christianity?,* it would be no less justified—and far closer to Harnack's stated intent—if one were to see in the lectures of 1899–1900 a distillate of the historical knoweldge that had already filled so many thousands of pages of his works by the turn of the century.[2]

While there is much to be said for Pelikan's observation, it is interesting to note that the definition of the essence of Christianity supplied by Harnack after his historical studies is similar to that supplied much earlier by Albrecht Ritschl in his historical and theological study of the doctrines of justification and reconciliation. Harnack stated that Christianity was no more than "the kingdom of God and its

2. *Ibid.,* p. 62.

coming. . . . God the Father and the infinite value of the human soul . . . [and] the higher righteousness and the commandment of love."[3] With more clarity Ritschl wrote:

> Christianity is the monotheistic, completely spiritual and ethical religion, which, based on the life of its author as Redeemer and as the founder of the kingdom of God, consists in the freedom of the children of God, involves the impulse to conduct from the motive of love, aims at the moral organisation of mankind, and grounds blessedness on the relation of sonship to God, as well as on the kingdom of God.[4]

This similarity suggests that Harnack actually approached the study of the history of dogma with certain Ritschlian presuppositions. This suggestion is strengthened by the fact that in a letter to Ritschl, which he sent with an advance copy of the first volume of the *History of Dogma,* Harnack wrote that "without the foundation which you laid, the *Dogmengeschichte* probably would never have been written."[5] Apart from emphasizing the centrality of the kingdom of God and its ethical aspects, Ritschl advanced the thesis that certain post-apostolic developments of Catholicism in the Gentile environment perverted the pure faith of the gospel. He also argued that the older Luther and his followers had distorted the initial vision of young Luther into the meaning of justification and reconciliation. In all three areas we can observe Ritschl's influence on Harnack.

In order to simplify our task of describing Harnack's theory of the development of dogma, I shall not primarily use the full *History* but rather its one-volume summary entitled *Outlines of the History of Dogma* (1893). First of all, however, we need to know how Harnack understood the word "dogma." He held that the church of the third and fourth centuries, having accepted a collection of writings and oral traditions as of divine origin, deduced from them a system of doctrine arranged in scientific form for apologetic

3. Quoted by G. W. Glick, *The Reality of Christianity: A Study of Adolf Von Harnack as Historian and Theologian* (New York: Harper & Row, 1967), p. 268.
4. A. Ritschl, *The Christian Doctrine of Justification and Reconciliation,* vol. 3 (Edinburgh, 1900), p. 13.
5. Quoted by Glick, *Reality of Christianity,* p. 53.

purposes. This system, which was imposed on the whole church, possessed those doctrines which explain the nature of God in Trinity and the Incarnation. Thus, as F. Loofs has observed, the *History of Dogma* is actually "a monograph on the rise and development of the dogma of the fourth century, written with genius and placed in a large context."[6] It was Harnack's contention that "the claim of the Church, that the dogmas are simply the exposition of the Christian revelation because deduced from the Holy Scripture, is not confirmed by historical investigation."[7] Furthermore, he believed that:

> . . . the history of dogma . . . offers the very best means and methods of freeing the Church from dogmatic Christianity and of hastening the inevitable progress of emancipation which began with Augustine. But the history of dogma testifies also to the unity and continuity of the Christian faith in the progress of its history, in so far as it proves that certain fundamental ideas of the Gospel have never been lost and have defied attacks.[8]

Following the Introduction, part one is divided into two sections: the preparation and the laying of the foundations. The period of preparation (c. 50–150) saw the decline of Jewish Christianity and the growth of syncretistic tendencies in Gentile Christian theology and worship. The latter were strengthened by the controversy with Gnosticism, whose teachers Harnack called the first real theologians: "They were the first to transform Christianity into a system of dogma; they were the first to work up the tradition systematically."[9] Their system, a philosophy of religions of the Greek spirit, was rejected by the great Church. However, the same spirit gradually prevailed even within the body which at first had rejected it. Between c. 150 and c. 260 there occurred:

> . . . the establishment of a great ecclesiastical society formed as a coterminous political community, school, and society for

6. Pelikan, *Historical Theology,* p. 61.
7. Harnack, *Outlines of the History of Dogma* (Scranton, PA: Beacon Press, 1957), p. 7.
8. *Ibid.,* pp. 7–8.
9. Quoted by Glick, *Reality of Christianity,* p. 134 (from the 3rd German edition of the *History of Dogma,* vol. 1, p. 215).

worship, and based on the strong foundation of an 'apostolic' law of faith, an 'apostolic' collection of writings and . . . an 'apostolic' organisation—in short the Catholic Church.[10]

Of decisive importance was the use of the *logos* concept in this Church by the apologists and especially by Origen. As Harnack explained:

> The establishment of the Logos-Christology within the faith of the Church—and indeed as *articulus fundamentalis*—was accomplished after severe conflicts during the course of a hundred years (till c. 300). It signified the transformation of the faith into a system of beliefs with an Hellenic-philosophical cast; it showed the old eschatological representations aside, and even suppressed them; . . . it gave the faith of the Christians a definite trend towards the contemplation of ideas and doctrinal formulas, and prepared the way, on the one side for the monastic life, and on the other for the chaperoned Christianity of the imperfect, active laity; it legitimized a hundred questions in metaphysics, cosmology and natural science as ecclesiastical. . . . (p. 167)

The *logos* concept thus became the catalytic agent for the development of an official scientific theology.

Part two is divided into three sections: the first surveys the development of the doctrine of the God-Man, the second examines the expansion and recasting of this central dogma into doctrines concerning sin and grace in medieval Augustinianism, and the third describes the threefold issuing of the history of dogma in the sixteenth century. The first builds upon the thesis that "through the acceptance of the Logos-Christology as the central dogma of the Church, the Church doctrine was firmly rooted in Hellenism." In it, Harnack seeks to show that the dogmas of the Nicene Creed and Chalcedonian Definition of the person of Christ do conform to this thesis. Origen and Athanasius are singled out for detailed treatment and it is shown that the influence of Origen, through his theological followers, gravitated towards the complete victory of philosophy over Christianity and of secularization over true faith. It was Athanasius who played a major role in arresting this development. Of him Harnack wrote:

10. *Ibid.*, vol. 1, p. 303.

He became the father of ecclesiastical orthodoxy and the pa-
tron of ecclesiastical monasticism: He taught nothing new; new
only was the doing, the energy and exclusiveness of his con-
ceptions and actions at a time when everything threatened to
dissolve. . . . He fixed a gulf between the Logos, of which the
philosophers thought, and the Logos, whose redeeming power
he proclaimed. That which he expressed concerning the latter,
while announcing the mystery emphatically and powerfully
and in no way indulging himself in new distinctions, appeared
to the Greeks an offence and foolishness. But he did not shun
this approach, rather did he circumscribe for the Christian
Faith within the already given speculation its own territory,
and thus did he find the way to ward off the complete hellenization and secularisation of Christianity. (p. 200)

Nevertheless, added Harnack, theological science came to a
standstill after the Council of Chalcedon.

In the second section of part two, Harnack tells us that
the history of dogma in the West from the fifth to the sixteenth century was determined by four elements: the Latin
theology of Tertullian, Cyprian, and Lactantius; the Hel-
lenic theology of the Nicene Creed; the Christianity of Augustine; and, to a lesser extent, the needs of the Romano-
Germanic nations. In Augustine, Harnack believed that he
found a man whose piety did not live in the old dogma, even
though he respected its authority and used it as building
material for his doctrine of religion: "Augustine in religion
discovered religion; he recognised his heart as the lowest,
and the living God as the highest good. . . . He rescued
religion from its communal and cultus form and restored it
to the heart as a gift and as a gracious life" (p. 336). It was,
however, not the warm piety but the cold dogma which
Augustine's successors received. They combined this with
Aristotelianism and the papal conception of the Church to
form scholasticism. At the close of the Middle Ages the
situation had so deteriorated that Harnack could claim that
"dogma is institution" and "dogma is a code of laws" (p. 503).

In the third section we learn that though various out-
comes seemed possible, those created from the crisis of the
early sixteenth century were Tridentine Catholicism,
Socinianism, and the Evangelical Reformation. All three

were burdened with contradictions. In the first the worst features of medieval theology and curialism were strengthened. As Tridentine Catholicism developed in the following centuries, the Roman Catholic Church revealed itself:

> ... as the autocratic dominion of the pontifex maximus—the old Roman Empire taking possession of the memory of Jesus Christ, founded upon his word and sacraments, exercising according to need an elastic or iron dogmatic legal discipline, encompassing purgatory and heaven in addition to earth. (p. 528)

The Radical Reformation, or Socinianism as Harnack called it, had for its presuppositions the great anti-ecclesiastical agitations of the Middle Ages. At the same time that it was nourished by the Renaissance and the Reformation, it was also a union of New Testament themes and rational religion. Using the tool of reason, it sought to cast aside the old teaching of the Catholic Church and return directly to the New Testament; however, in rejecting the old dogma it created a new one.

For the evangelical Reformation—Luther in particular —Harnack reserved his praises (as well as a large number of pages).

> Luther restored the religious view of the Gospel, the sovereign worth of the historical Person, Jesus Christ, in Christianity. In doing this he went back beyond the Church of the Middle Ages and the old Catholic times to the New Testament, yes, to the Gospel itself. But the very man who freed the Gospel of Jesus Christ from ecclesiasticism and moralism strengthened the force of the latter under the forms of the old Catholic theology, yes, he gave to these forms which for centuries had lain dormant, once again a value and a meaning. He was the restorer of the old dogmas and he gave them back to faith. One must credit it to him that these formulas are even until today a living power in the faith of Protestantism, while in the Catholic Churches they are a dead weight. (p. 542)

But Luther only made a beginning. The most important confusions and problems in his legacy to Protestantism were the following: the confounding of the gospel and the "doctrina evangelii"; the confounding of evangelical faith and old dogma; and the confounding of grace and the means of grace. Therefore, it was the task of theologians to finish the work Luther began. In *Das Wesen des Christentums* Harnack felt he was doing just this. As he once wrote:

> We study history in order to intervene in the course of history and we have a right and duty so to do; for without historical knowledge we remain either passive objects of development or we mislead people irresponsibly. . . . Only that knowledge which serves for the present has a right to demand that it become the subject of knowledge for us.[11]

In this statement Harnack reminds us that when he wrote history he did so in order to inspire men to know the bare facts as well as to become enlightened Christians in their own generation. Many today would say that this is not a realistic aim.

The literature on the truth or falsity of Harnack's theory of Hellenization is immense. My own view is that both Harnack's theory and the modern one set forth by Leslie Dewart in *The Future of Belief* (1966) are mistaken. The composers of the Nicene Creed were far more concerned to protect Christian thought from Hellenization than to Hellenize it![12]

James Orr (1844–1913)

Born in Glasgow, James Orr lost his parents when he was only a boy. This delayed his formal education and it was not until he was twenty-three that he became a student at Glasgow University. After graduating Master of Arts, he studied theology at the United Presbyterian Divinity Hall and took the Glasgow Bachelor of Divinity degree in 1871. After twenty years as a parish minister, he moved in 1891 to become Professor of Church History in the United Presbyterian Divinity Hall. The book which brought him fame, par-

11. Quoted by Glick, *Reality of Christianity,* p. 108 from Harnack, *Reden und Aufsatze,* band IV, pp. 7–9.
12. For a summary of the criticisms made of Harnack's theory of the development of dogma see Glick, *Reality of Christianity,* pp. 143ff. On the question of the dehellenization of dogma, I find Bernard Lonergan's work helpful. See his "The Dehellenization of Dogma," in *New Theology No. 5,* ed. M. E. Marty and D. G. Peerman (New York: Macmillan, 1968).

ticularly in North America, was his *The Christian View of God and the World* (1893). In 1897, he gave the Elliott Lectures at the Western Theological Seminary, Allegheny, and published them four years later as *The Progress of Dogma*. On the same visit to America he lectured at Auburn Theological Seminary, giving the Morgan Lectures on the Early Church. These appeared as *Neglected Factors in the Study of the Early Progress of Christianity* (1899).

In 1900, he became Professor of Apologetics and Dogmatics in the new Trinity College, Glasgow, and he remained here until his death. His colleagues included George Adam Smith in Old Testament, James Denney in New Testament, and Thomas M. Lindsay in Church History. Orr's obituary in the *British Weekly* of September 11, 1913, stated:

> Dr. Orr was a laborious worker and the range of his first-hand knowledge was immense. He did not speak about men like Kant and Hegel . . . Schleiermacher and Ritschl, Spencer and Darwin, from hearsay or on the strength or compendiums; he had mastered them in their own writings and his mind was massive enough to weigh them in its own scales and to be its own authority upon them.

Most of his writings were addressed to theological students, ministers, and educated laity, and thus were not written at the same academic level as some of the books (e.g., Harnack's *History of Dogma*) he was answering.[13]

In the preface to *The Progress of Dogma,* there is a clue to his general aim in the series of lectures:

> Their object will be gained if the conviction is implanted that here also [in doctrine] 'an increasing purpose' runs 'through the ages', and that the labour spent by myriads of minds on the fashioning of dogma, has not, as so many in our day seem to think, been utterly fatuous, and the mere forging of fetters for the human spirit.

He was very much aware that many Germans and Americans were teaching that doctrine and dogma were unnecessary.

---

13. For a brief study of Orr's life see P. Toon, "James Orr: Defender of the Faith," *The Gospel Magazine* (August 1972). There is a thesis on Orr by A. P. Neely in the Library of the Southern Baptist Seminary at Fort Worth, Texas.

The first lecture, in which he stated his theory of development, is fundamental for the whole series. In the remaining nine lectures, he illustrated his theory by examples from the history of doctrine. He desired to examine how dogma has been shaped in history, to ascertain what law has guided its development, and to inquire into its abiding value. This examination involved opposing such scholars as Harnack, who regarded the actual history of dogma as a pathological rather than a normal or healthy process, and others, who applied the theory of evolution to Christianity in such a way that the faith of the early Church was merely at a kindergarten level as compared with that of the nineteenth-century Church.

As a result of such attacks, there was some question regarding the future of dogma in the Church. As Orr stated: "Must theology, whose daughter 'dogma' is, in face of these hostile forces, vacate her throne, and resign her pretensions to have any sure and verifiable results to lay before men?" Often, he regretted the affirmative answer given by his contemporaries. They saw little purpose or future in doctrine; their interest was in morality. His own reply was as follows:

> While conscious, I hope, of the limits of thought on such a subject, I believe, as I have always done, that there is a place and need for doctrinal theology; that there is a truth, or sum of truths, involved in the Biblical revelation, for which it is the duty of the Church to bear witness; that Christianity is not something utterly formless and vague, but has an ascertainable, statable content, which it is the business of the Church to find out, to declare, to defend, and ever more perfectly to seek to unfold in the connection of its parts, and in relation to advancing knowledge; that this content of truth is not something that can be manipulated into any shape men's fancies please, but something in regard to which we should not despair of being able to arrive at a large measure of agreement, if, indeed, the Protestant Churches have not already so arrived. I believe also, with more direct relation to our present subject, that, so far from the history of dogma being the fatuous, illusory thing that many people suppose, there is a true law and logic underlying its progress, a true divine purpose and leading in its developments, a deeper and more complete understanding of Christianity in its many-sided relations

being wrought out by its labours; and that, while its advance has not been without much conflict, much error, much implication with human sin and infirmity, and is yet far from complete, that advance has in the main been onward, and has yielded results which further progress will not subvert, any more than the future developments of science will subvert, say, such discoveries as the circulation of the blood, or the law of gravitation. (pp. 8–9)

In the general climate of Christendom at that time, this amounted to a very positive affirmation, and he was aware that many would see it as utterly extravagant. If, as Orr believed, the history of dogma presented an analogous advance to scientific progress, then he felt he had to assert this in his day when everything theological was "being flung into the melting-pot, and doctrines, torn from their context in history and the system of faith" were often treated in the most arbitrary manner.

At this point Orr entered into definitions of doctrine (the direct, often naive, expression by Christians of the knowledge they have or convictions they hold), of theology (the reflective exercise of the mind on the doctrines of the Faith), and dogma (formulations of doctrine which have obtained authoritative recognition in wide sections of the Church), in order to argue against Harnack regarding the definition of dogma. Orr wanted to elevate the major doctrines of the Protestant churches to the status of dogma. As the title of his book indicates, he did this; and thus, some of his lectures are concerned with Protestant dogma as well as Catholic dogma.

Having clarified the dogma which he intended to portray and defend, he was able to begin introducing his theory. He did this by raising the question of tests designed to ascertain the truth or falsity of a particular dogma or system of dogma. As a Protestant, he could not wholly submit to Councils or Synods, to an infallible Pope or, with the rationalist, to human reason. He could, however, gladly submit to the authority of Scripture; however, most if not all disputants appealed to Scripture, and this made it difficult to claim that Scripture favored one or the other. There were other tests, though. For example, is the system of dogma an organic unity? Do the doctrines harmonize with the religious experience of the saints through the centuries? Do the practical results issuing from the dogma glorify God? Again, though useful, these tests did not eliminate the subjective element. There was need for an objective criterion.

Orr recognized that a truly objective criterion was not available, but he believed that he had come close to it in the method he adopted in the lectures—"that of appeal to the rigorous, impartial . . . the practically unerring verdict of history." The history of dogma was the judgment of dogma.

> One thing I am absolutely persuaded of, that, whatever imperfections inhere in our existing creeds, no phase of doctrine which the Church has with full deliberation rejected—which, on each occasion of its reappearance, it has persisted in rejecting—need raise its head now with any hope of permanent acceptance. And this principle alone, as we shall see, carries us a long way. The history of dogma criticises dogma; corrects mistakes, eliminates temporary elements, supplements defects, incorporates the gains of the past, at the same time that it opens up wider horizons for the future. But its clock never goes back. It never returns upon itself to take up as part of its creed what it has formally, and with full consciousness, rejected at some bygone stage. (p. 17)

In other words, there had been real progress in theology over the centuries.

To explain this progress he used the model of evolution; interestingly, Orr believed in theistic evolution: "I plant myself here," he wrote, "on the most modern of all doctrines—the doctrine of evolution, supposed by many to be fatal to the permanence of dogma" (p. 18). In granting that there had been an evolution of dogma, Orr was running the risk of giving the impression that the later dogma was superior to the earlier. To counteract this he wrote:

> Genuine evolution illustrates a law of continuity. It is not a violent breaking with preceding forms, but proves its legitimacy by its capability of fitting into a development already, perhaps, in large measure accomplished. In like manner, the test of a sound theological development is not its independence of what has gone before, but the degree of its respect for it, the depth of its insight into it, and its capacity of uniting itself with it, and carrying it a stage further towards completion. (pp. 19–20)

It was fundamental to this argument that evolution was homogeneous development.

At this point, Orr introduced Newman's principles of development in order to state his agreement with them. However, because of their generality they were of little help. It was not the general principles of evolution in history, but rather "the immanent law of the actual history" which would furnish him with a corroboration—a *rationale*—for the basic evangelical Protestant dogma.

One sure way to recognize the immanent law was to note "what a singular *parallel* there is between the historical course of dogma, on the one hand, and the scientific order of the text-books on systematic theology on the other":

> The history of dogma, as you speedily discover, is simply the system of theology spread out through the centuries— theology, as Plato would say, "writ large"—and this not only as regards its general subject-matter, but even as respects the definite succession of its parts. The temporal and the logical order correspond. The articulation of the system in your textbooks is the very articulation of the system in its development in history. Take, for example, any accredited theological textbook, and observe the order of its treatment. What we ordinarily find is something like this. Its opening sections are probably occupied with matters of Theological Prolegomena—with apologetics, the general idea of religion, revelation, the relation of faith to reason, Holy Scripture, and the like. Then follow the great divisions of the theological system—Theology proper, or the doctrine of God; Anthropology, or the doctrine of man, including sin (sometimes a separate division); Christology, or the doctrine of the Person of Christ; Soteriology (Objective), or the doctrine of the work of Christ, especially the Atonement; Subjective Soteriology, or the doctrine of the application of redemption (Justification, Regeneration, etc.); finally, Eschatology, or the doctrine of the last things. If now, planting yourself at the close of the Apostolic Age, you cast your eye down the course of the succeeding centuries, you find, taking as an easy guide the great historical controversies of the Church, that what you have is simply the projection of this logical system on a vast temporal screen. (pp. 21–22)

The immanent law of history was the logical law of the systematic theologians.

Orr was aware that books on systematic theology could and did present doctrines in various orders—some began with man and his sin, others with Christ. Yet, he maintained that the order in which he had listed the doctrines or topics was the order of logical sequence and dependence. And in a survey of the emergence of dogma in Church history (of which later lectures were a grand expansion) he demonstrated that the logical order was in fact, quite remarkably, the very order in which doctrines were debated and clarified. In fact, all basic dogma, except eschatology, had emerged—and he expected his own generation or the next to clarify this area.

Therefore he could summarize his theory:

> The development is not arbitrary, but shaped by the inner reason and necessity of the case. The simple precedes the more complex; fundamental doctrines those which need the former as their basis; problems in the order in which they naturally and inevitably arise in the evolution of thought.

It could appear from what has been said that Orr viewed the accumulated dogma as fixed and final, but this would be a misinterpretation, for he wrote:

> Existing systems are not final; as works of human understanding they are necessarily imperfect; there is none which is not in some degree affected by the nature of the intellectual environment, and the factors the mind had, at the time of formulation, to work with. I do not question, therefore, that there are sides and aspects of divine truth to which full justice has not yet been accorded; improvements that can be made in our conception and formulation of all the doctrines, and in their correlation with each other. All I am contending for is, that such a development shall be a development *within* Christianity and not *away* from it; that it shall recognise its connection with the past, and unite organically with it; and it shall not spurn the past development, as if nothing of permanent value had been accomplished by it. (pp. 30–31)

Here, as he clarified in the lectures, he demonstrates his awareness of the humanity of doctrine relative to the language (e.g., Greek or Latin) in which it was originally expressed, and relative to the philosophical vocabulary available to the theologian (e.g., *ousia* for those at the Council of Nicea). At the same time he recognizes the guidance of God in the Church through history, and he expresses this conviction relative to an immanent law of logic.

To survey the remaining nine lectures would be a laborious task and would achieve little. The following are the general themes of the remaining lectures:

Lecture Two　Early apologetic and fundamental religious ideas—controversy with paganism and Gnosticism (second century).

Lecture Three　The doctrine of God; Trinity and deity of Son and Spirit—Monarchian, Arian, and Macedonian controversies (third and fourth centuries).

Lecture Four　Continuation of themes of the third lecture.

Lecture Five　The doctrine of man and sin; grace and predestination—Augustinian and Pelagian controversy (fifth century).

Lecture Six　The doctrine of the person of Christ—the Christological controversies: Apollinarian, Nestorian, Eutychian, Monophysite, Monothelite (fifth to seventh centuries).

Lecture Seven　The doctrine of the Atonement—Anselm and Abelard to the Reformation (eleventh to sixteenth centuries).

Lecture Eight　The doctrine of the application of Redemption; Justification by faith; Regeneration, etc.— Protestantism and Roman Catholicism (sixteenth century).

Lecture Nine　Post-Reformation theology: Lutheranism and Calvinism—new influences acting on theology and their results in rationalism (seventeenth and eighteenth centuries).

Lecture Ten　Modern restatement of the problems of theology—the doctrine of the last things (nineteenth century).

Orr's theory appeals to those who believe in the providence of God working for the Church of Christ and to those who value both Catholic and Protestant formulations in the ecumenical and reformational creeds. Yet it can be questioned on both sides. The logical sequence which he believed to be so obvious and beyond dispute is hardly so. The chapters of the Westminster Confession of Faith do not, for example, exactly correspond to the sequence favored by Orr. Neither do the various headings and books of the *Summa Theologica* of Aquinas (which, apart from anything else, was a great logical presentation). Then the maintenance of historical sequence requires a selective reading and ordering of the way in which dogma emerged.[14] Orr does not deal with the emergence of the doctrine of the Church, ministry, and sacraments. Therefore, Orr laid himself open to the charge that while Newman opted for an infallible Pope, he opted for an infallible, logical law.

Regarding Harnack, Orr answered him only to the extent of proposing a totally different theory to explain the relation of Church dogma to Scripture and other dogma. In the lectures on the Church of the first five centuries, there are many references to Harnack at points where Orr is disagreeing with him. However, Orr's treatment of the patristic period is too brief, in comparison with that of Harnack, to become a true reply or answer to Harnack.

Benjamin B. Warfield (1851–1921)

As an appendix to his book, Orr printed a long extract from an essay by Warfield on "The right of systematic theology." Since Warfield is still, to a greater extent than Orr, highly respected by evangelicals for his vigorous presentation of Calvinistic orthodoxy, it will be instructive to note his views on development. He did not treat the subject of development at any length, but he gave a summary of his views in the essay "The idea of systematic theology" in his *Studies in Theology* (1932). For him, theology was an inductive study of facts conveyed in a written revelation. So there could be, and had been, a true progression in theology

---

14. Here the reader may compare the arrangement of Orr with that of Jaroslav Pelikan in *The Christian Tradition, A History of the Development of Doctrine* (vol. 1, 1971). Pelikan discusses the person of Christ before he discusses "Nature and Grace." So also does J. N. D. Kelly in his *Early Christian Doctrine* (4th ed., 1976).

in that there had been progress in "gathering, defining, mentally assimilating and organizing these facts into a correlated system." He wrote:

> The affirmation that theology has been a progressive science is no more, then, than to assert that it is a science that has had a history—and a history which can be and should be genetically traced and presented. First, the objective side of Christian truth was developed: pressed on the one side by the crass monotheism of the Jews and on the other by the coarse polytheism of the heathen, and urged on by its own internal need of comprehending the sources of its life, Christian theology first searched the Scriptures that it might understand the nature and modes of existence of its God and the person of its divine Redeemer. Then, more and more conscious of itself, it more and more fully wrought out from those same Scriptures a guarded expression of the subjective side of its faith; until through throes and conflicts it has built up the system which we all inherit. Thus the body of Christian truth has come down to us in the form of an organic growth; and we can conceive of the completed structure as the ripened fruit of the ages, as truly as we can think of it as the perfected result of the exegetical discipline. As it has come into our possession by this historic process, there is no reason that we can assign why it should not continue to make for itself a history. We do not expect the history of theology to close in our own day. However nearly completed our realization of the body of truth may seem to us to be; however certain it is that the great outlines are already securely laid and most of the details soundly discovered and arranged; no one will assert that every detail is as yet perfected, and we are all living in the confidence so admirably expressed by old John Robinson, "that God hath more truth yet to break forth from His holy Word." Just because God gives us the truth in single threads which we must weave into the reticulated texture, all the threads are always within our reach, but the finished texture is ever and will ever continue to be before us until we dare affirm that there is no truth in the Word which we have not perfectly apprehended, and no relation of these truths as revealed which we have not perfectly understood, and no possibility in clearness of presentation which we have not attained. (pp. 77–78)

To illustrate his view of progress of doctrine he gave two examples, neither of which is very helpful. The first was the building of one of the great medieval cathedrals. This task was not the work of one architect and one generation of workmen, but each generation took over where a previous one had left off. Yet, they all had worked together to produce the one cathedral. Warfield would have made this into a better example had he stated, as no doubt he knew, that sometimes there was demolition (by storm, fire, or intent) before a further stage of the building progress took place. The demolition then would have illustrated that in the history of dogma there have been erroneous elements which have to be removed.

The second example was that of laying a railroad across a continent (an experience which nineteenth-century Americans knew well). This was accomplished by the "simple process of laying each rail at the end of the line already laid." This also is a poor example. The actual history of the formulation of doctrine in the Church from the Council of Nicea in 325 to the Diet of Worms in 1521 contained the promulgation and acceptance of many doctrines (on Church, ministry, sacraments, purgatory, etc.) which Warfield was not prepared to accept. But, in his illustration, they were some of the rails which made up the railway track. The same, of course, can be said of the example of the cathedral, for the doctrinal work of the Reformers and the Protestant theologians who followed them included the demolition of the major part of the structure of the "cathedral" theology of the Middle Ages which they inherited.

All the models or illustrative analogies used by Orr and Warfield are unsatisfactory either because the two men appear not to have used the model/analogy fairly or because their model/analogy is unsatisfactory. The last point is illustrated by my comments above on the cathedral and railroad. On the first point, my criticism is that the model of homogeneous evolution or development, be it based on the biological doctrine of evolution or the progress of knowledge in any of the natural sciences, is not applied consistently by either man. They are both extremely selective concerning what they will accept as right doctrine in the Church of the period both before and after the Council of Chalcedon to the time of Luther.[15] I am not saying that the two men were wrong in rejecting as unfaithful to Scripture certain medieval doctrines; rather, I am saying that their models required them to take account of the development of theology as theology (whether they judged it sound or false) and this they did not do.

15. To illustrate this point I invite the reader to examine the topics covered in Jaroslav Pelikan's second and third volumes of *The Christian Tradition* (1974 and 1978), and then compare that list of doctrines with the few topics allowed by Orr and Warfield from this period of Church history.

CHAPTER FIVE

RECENT PROTESTANT THEOLOGY

THE DEVELOPMENT of doctrine has not been seen as a major issue in Protestantism because doctrinal development is not regarded by Protestants as issuing in infallible dogma as in Roman Catholicism. For Protestants, only Scripture (or "revelation" as some prefer) is finally authoritative and infallible. The Roman Catholic starts with doctrine (e.g., Mariology) which goes beyond what is explicitly taught in the Bible, and he then attempts to reconcile this doctrine with the Bible. Beginning with the belief in the authority of Scripture, the *sola scriptura*, the Protestant must interpret the *sola* so as not to exclude the development of doctrine in the Church and the giving of a secondary authority to confessions of faith. Therefore, much attention within Protestantism has been focused on the Bible in order to decide its value for the Church today.

Unity and Diversity in the New Testament

It is certainly true that there has been a very important progression in the doctrine of Scripture within the Protestant academic community over the last century. Whether we call this "development" or "corruption" will depend on how well we understand it and its implications. Very few modern theologians hold to a view of verbal inspiration and most see the books of the Bible as essentially human products which act as human witnesses to revelation. They point to revelation, they record human understanding of revelation, but they are not divinely-guaranteed accounts of revelation. This progression in doctrine can easily be seen by reading what James Barr, an Oxford Professor in Old Testament, says about evangelical and older Protestant views in his *Fundamentalism* (1977). Barr's commitment to the "historical method" (understanding books only in their context) appears to be unqualified, and though he accuses evangelicals of failing to be self-critical in their (according to him) naive views of Scripture, he also, like so many modern theologians, seems not to have considered that liberals ought also to be self-critical of their presuppositions. Only in a few cases, however, has this modern approach to Scripture, dominated by "the historical method," been put into a credal form. Perhaps the best example is in the last confession in the *Book of Confessions* (1967) of the United Presbyterian Church. So, within this context of contemporary study of the Bible, particularly of the New Testament, let us note aspects regarding our theme.

Questions about the development of doctrine in the early Christian communities and reflected in the New Testament as well as the variety of teaching within the same Testament have been widely discussed.[1] Discussion on a variety of theologies such as Johannine, Pauline, and Lucan is now common even in evangelical seminaries.[2] Less common in such seminaries is the speculation among modern scholars of developments in Christian teaching which are now embodied in the New Testament. One such development is giving of the title "Lord" (Kyrios) to the Messiah, Jesus of Nazareth, by the Gentile Christian communities.[3] Another

1. For details see W. G. Kümmel, *The New Testament: The History of the Investigation of its Problems* (Nashville: Abingdon, 1972).
2. See G. E. Ladd, *A Theology of the New Testament* (Grand Rapids: Eerdmans, 1974).
3. There is much literature on this topic but see W. Bousset, *Kyrios Christos* (1921); Oscar Cullmann, *The Christology of the New Testament* (London: SCM, 1963; Philadelphia: Westminster, 1964); and I. H. Marshall, *The Origins of New Testament Christology* (Downers Grove, IL: Inter-Varsity, 1977).

is the possible restatement of eschatological teaching after the realization that there would not be an immediate return of Christ.[4]

In addition to these questions of variety and development are questions concerning the kind of unity the New Testament possesses and how its books are to be interpreted.[5] Hermeneutics is a word which we hear and read everywhere, and the literature on the subject is growing at a tremendous rate.[6] Thus, what was a fairly settled, divinely authoritative basis for faith and practice for our forefathers has become the center of much critical discussion. Observing this, evangelicals have felt that the whole tribe of modern biblical scholars is intent on destroying the authority of the Bible. Naturally, in this situation, evangelical scholars have felt it necessary to devote their energies not only towards maintaining a full doctrine of the inspiration of Scripture, but also towards discussing questions of hermeneutics and development within the New Testament. A glance through the annual lists of publications of the members of the evangelical Tyndale Fellowship (centered at Tyndale House, Cambridge) will amply prove this point.

Only a limited amount of Protestant intellectual energy has been put into discussing the problems of the development of doctrine. If there is, after all, no infallible basis for faith, or we cannot be sure what our possible infallible basis means, why should we bother to investigate

4. R. Bultmann justified his own reinterpretation of the teaching of the New Testament on the basis that the writer of John's Gospel reinterpreted the idea of the *parousia* of the Son of Man relative to Christ coming in the Spirit to believers. See his *Commentary on John* (Philadelphia: Westminster, 1971) and his exegesis of 5:25–29 and 14:1–14. C. H. Dodd, the British scholar, also believed that there was a change in eschatology and spoke of a realized eschatology. See his *The Interpretation of the Fourth Gospel* (New York: Cambridge Univ. Press, 1958). Among scholars who continue the tradition of Bultmann are Ebeling, Bornkamm, James Robinson, Fuchs, Schmithals, and Conzelmann.
5. For discussion of unity and diversity see H. Conzelmann, *Outline of the Theology of the New Testament* (New York: Harper & Row, 1969); J. Jeremias, *New Testament Theology* (New York: Scribner, 1971); and W. G. Kümmel, *The Theology of the New Testament* (Nashville: Abingdon, 1973; London: SCM, 1974).
6. See further I. H. Marshall, ed., *New Testament Interpretation: Essays on Principles and Methods* (Grand Rapids: Eerdmans, 1977).

dogma, for one man's opinion will be as good as another's! It is not merely accidental that only a small proportion of doctoral theses accepted by British university theology departments have been on theology proper, that is, on dogmatic or systematic theology.[7] Often, we have to deduce what modern theologians think about development of doctrine from their statements on the interpretation and relevance of the New Testament, Scripture and tradition, and the basis for Church unity. On the last point, the development of doctrine becomes an issue when denominations with powerful traditions (e.g., Anglicanism, Presbyterianism, and Lutheranism) discuss the possibility of union.

Creeds and Confessions

Before discussing how contemporary theologians view development, it would be helpful to recall how the Protestant Reformers understood the relation of Church dogma/doctrine to Scripture in order to see why we today cannot adopt their understanding without major qualifications. They saw their own confessions of faith or books on basic doctrines as mere summaries or compendia of Scripture teaching. Yet, these confessions and books contained not only their own doctrines of penal, substitutionary atonement and justification by faith, but also the old Church dogma of the Trinity and the person of Christ. They were not aware of what we call the development of doctrine. Working with the rule that Scripture is its own interpreter, they were able, by explaining the obscure or difficult parts by the clearer, to produce remarkable and consistent doctrinal interpretations of the entire Bible. In seventeenth-century orthodoxy—be it Lutheran, Reformed, or Anglican—this procedure continued as witnessed by such statements as the Westminster Confession and the Canons of the Synod of Dordt (1618).

Virtually all modern scholars now agree that these confessions of faith are not simply distillations of biblical theol-

---

7. E. J. Burge, "Recent Higher Degrees in Theology," *Theology,* lxviii (1965), pp. 431ff. Not much has changed since 1965.

ogy translated into a modern European language. With the wealth of historical studies available to us, we cannot regard the doctrinal formulations of the Reformation period as mere summaries of what God had said through all the writers of the Bible. For example, Articles VI and VII of the Belgic Confession, which deal with canonical and apocryphal books and their authority, are not summaries of biblical teaching but beliefs about the Bible, stated against the claims of Roman Catholicism. Other teaching in this Confession demonstrates the errors of Pelagianism (e.g., Article XIV) and the Anabaptists (e.g., Article XXXVI). Then, of course, the Confession uses the language of the Catholic creeds on the doctrines of the Trinity and person of Christ.

Over the centuries the consensus of theological inquiry has confirmed the correctness of this interpretative "extra"; but there are modern theologians who would challenge it and say that it is not the only "valid" interpretation of Christian revelation available to us. For example, it has recently been claimed that "our Trinity of revelation is an arbitrary analysis of the activity of God, which though of value in Christian thought and devotion is not of essential significance."[8] Then, in the field of Christology the Chalcedonian Definition (the main points of which are incorporated in the Athanasian Creed) is attacked as being too emphatic in the "two nature" doctrine.[9]

Historical Situationalism

Perhaps the most powerful factor, apart from contemporary biblical exegesis, causing modern theologians to question or to reject the Catholic dogma, as well as to reject such Protestant doctrine as the penal, substitutionary atonement, is what is usually called "historical situationalism." The best way to illustrate this in regard to the formation of doctrine is the model of the inter-action of

8. M. Wiles, *Working Papers in Doctrine* (Naperville, IL: Allenson, 1976), p. 15.
9. *Ibid.*, pp. 122ff.; A. T. Hanson, *Grace and Truth. A Study in the Doctrine of the Incarnation* (London: SPCK, 1975); and J. A. T. Robinson, *The Human Face of God* (Philadelphia: Westminster, 1973).

the structured elements with the constituent elements. An example of this model from modern industrial life would be the production line in a factory. Various materials, semi-processed, enter the production line at one end. As they move along they are molded or pressed by men and their machines until the final product emerges at the end. The structured elements (metals, plastics, etc.) inter-act or fuse with the constituent elements (the activity of men and their machines) to produce something.

This model can be used to understand the theological work of the Westminister Assembly between 1643 and 1647. An assembly of British, "Calvinist" theologians, called into existence by Parliament (which was at war with the King), sought first to revise the Thirty-Nine Articles and then, at Parliament's command, produced a new Confession and Catechisms. Most of the men in the assembly were learned men, diligent students of the Scriptures. They gleaned from the Scriptures what they believed to be obvious teaching on a wide variety of topics. Yet, in reading and interpreting the Bible, they could not help but read it as men of the mid-seventeenth century who belonged to a specific Protestant tradition. In translating into the English language and contemporary thought-forms that which they believed to be Scripture, they were obviously affected by the recent controversies which many of them had engaged in—controversies with Roman Catholicism, Arminianism, and Anglican high-church principles. Thus, their Confession and their Catechisms are the result of the interaction of the structured elements—doctrinal ideas read from Scripture—with the constituent elements—the English language, the conceptual framework of their day, and the controversial questions of the period. The most obvious examples of this are the chapters on the Sabbath (ch. XXI) and the Civil Magistrate (XXIII); the latter was changed by American Presbyterians.

Now this model does not indicate how "faithful to Scripture" the Westminster divines were. It merely highlights that they did their theological thinking and writing in a specific context and that context had some effect on the way they read and interpreted the Bible as well as expressed its teaching. It is the task of the historian to point out the possibilities of expression and formulation rejected in, or not considered by, the men in the assembly, and it is the task of the theologian to decide whether the contents of the Westminster standards have validity, in whole or part, for today's Church.

Aware that all Church and denominational doctrine is historically and culturally conditioned, most modern scholars reject all views of development which portray it as merely a continuous, cumulative growth in understanding revelation.[10] The homogeneous evolution of dogma favored by Orr and Warfield is not seriously considered as an adequate explanation. Doctrine is seen as a historically conditioned response by the Church to questions put to her at a particular time and place by the world or by her members. Thus, the answers of one generation are not always of use to another, because culture, language, and questions change. Therefore, development of doctrine can be understood relative to the continuity of aims—the aims being to state the Faith in the best way (being faithful to Scripture, the nature of worship, and the experience of salvation) for each generation and in each culture. This form of understanding allows for differences of theological formulation at different times and in different countries. Another way of understanding development is by a question-answering exercise. The Church creates doctrine as she responds to questions which the world forces upon her, or to the obviously erroneous teaching of some of her members. Since doctrine is so obviously conditioned by the environment in which it was created, today it is usually also claimed that, while the Scriptures remain the primary source of doctrine, the historical situation makes a significant contribution relative to providing the language and the concepts available to the theologians and relative to the way in which the questions are asked. For example, for the Western Church to formu-

10. See M. Wiles, *The Making of Christian Doctrine* (New York: Cambridge Univ. Press, 1967) and *The Remaking of Christian Doctrine* (Naperville, IL: Allenson, 1974).

late a doctrine of man for today means using a language like English or German, adopting terminology which probably has specific meaning within the behavioral sciences, relating to the way in which human beings are understood in our culture (and this involves both the presuppositions of individuality and freedom with which most people work and the sophisticated theories of philosophers), as well as seeking to understand what the Scriptures teach and what the Church of the past has taught.

We are constantly reminded that appeals to the past can be either dangerous or helpful. If we merely reproduce the statements of the past in the present, then we are in danger of teaching misleading doctrine. Having taught the meaning of the Nicene and Athanasian Creeds, I know the force of this point. Many Anglican laity and ordinands have strange ideas as to the meaning of such words as "substance," "person," and "nature" in the creeds. We are urged to reassess the meaning of revelation so that we can speak realistically to modern men. Of course, to know the way in which men of old formulated their doctrine of God or Christ will probably help in the process of reassessing our own doctrine. Thus, the ancient creeds should function as signposts guiding the contemporary Church in its search for answers to modern questions about God, or in some cases, as buoys warning us to keep clear of dangerous "theological" rocks.

In summary, while modern theologians emphasize the reality of the continuity of the Church in history, they do not understand that continuity in terms which give the impression of merely homogeneous development of either doctrine or worship. Recent studies of the relation of Scripture and tradition, especially that study produced by the Montreal Conference on Faith and Order of 1964, clearly indicate this.[11] The general views held today regarding the progress in doctrine can probably best be expressed by two illustrative models. The first highlights the different understandings which arise from viewing and responding to one and the same object from different perspectives and circumstances.

11. P. C. Rodger and L. Vischer, eds., *Fourth World Conference on Faith and Order* (New York: Association Press, 1964).

Take the different ways in which it is possible to understand and respond to a play about life in Soweto, the South African township. As a person who has been to Soweto I can read it in my armchair; a racist or liberal European can watch it when performed in London or Stockholm; blacks can go to a production of it by an amateur company in a small town in Mississippi or can see it on Broadway; or the Bantu (as white South Africans call them) can see it performed in their townships or homelands. Likewise Christians of different centuries and cultures can see the contents of the Bible from different perspectives and with different emotions and questions.

The second model is probably a better one, for it uses the word "development," which, as stated in the Introduction, is a word with which we are saddled. This model is the development of a building site (a very common expression—at least in the United Kingdom). The developer buys a site on which may be a grand old house or just dilapidated buildings. According to prior plans, he develops the site either by removing all the old buildings and erecting new ones, or by renewing the old through demolition, restructuring, and renovation. The completed development could then last for centuries or for only a few decades.

This model illustrates that development of doctrine is not an organic, regular growth but rather a complex one. Historical research indicates that theology has often been diverted into a wrong path along which it has traveled for centuries and therefore needs either radical restatement (as at the Reformation) or major adjustments. The model also highlights the significance of the developer—the Athanasius or the Luther who stands *contra mundum*. It also illustrates that development reflects the time when it occurred (architectural style and materials used) and so points to the historical situationalism of all doctrine.

New Confessions?

Thus, with the general agreement that historical situationalism has to be taken seriously, it has followed that there is a reluctance in the major denominations to use the creeds or confessions of the past as tests of orthodoxy or heresy for today. An obvious example of this tendency is that the Church of England appears not to be taking any disciplinary action against those who, as contributors to the book *The Myth of God Incarnate* (ed. J. Hick, 1977), denied the classic Christological doctrine of the Nicene and Athanasian Creeds (as well as of Articles I and II of the Thirty-Nine Articles). This refusal to take action against what seems to most ordinary clergy and laity (who are generally conservative with respect to that theology which they think they understand) to be heresy, brings regrettable confusion and anxiety in the ordinary parish congregations. (No doubt the same is the case in similar matters in congregations in North America.) In defending themselves, the theologians who wrote in, or commend this volume, usually point to the supposed diversity of theological portrayals of Christ (or of other realities) in the Bible as the basis for a variety of views within the Church of today. Therefore, where this kind of thinking is influential in ecumenical circles and in the World Council of Churches, the plea is made for the legitimacy of a variety of ways of stating the Christian faith. This variety relates to confessions of faith in different languages, produced by the Church in many cultures, as well as confessions from the different denominational traditions in Europe and North America. Such a position is not surprising, for many scholars view the Bible as a collection of *human* witnesses to divine revelation.

Strange as it may seem, however, there is a general consensus that it is sometimes necessary to produce "emergency" statements of faith, as ecumenically-based as possible, designed to meet contemporary needs or situations. *The Declaration of Barmen* (1934), produced by the Confessional Synod of the German Evangelical Church and addressed to the Christians of Germany in the face of the threat from National Socialism, is often quoted as an example. Usually these "emergency" statements are produced by Councils of Churches (e.g., the British Council of Churches) and are concerned with issues such as racism, apartheid, totalitarian communism, and economic and social evils. Theoretically at least, those who call for such statements see them as historically and culturally conditioned!

One further interesting development of doctrine which is occurring in those denominations which are affiliated to the World Council is the emerging agreement that in future, united denominations the ministry of the Church should be that of the historic episcopate with the threefold ministry of bishop, presbyter, and deacon. Here there is commitment not to a biblical doctrine, arrived at after careful exegesis and interpretation, but to a universal tradition of Christendom from the second to the sixteenth century, and, since then, in some of the branches of Christendom. As an Anglican, I am grateful for this move in (what appears to me) the right direction as far as the ministry of the Church is concerned, but I am fearful that if one major principle can be allowed on the basis of tradition (yet, I think in this instance, tradition which does not deny any Scriptural principle), then others, possibly erroneous ones, will be admitted on non-scriptural grounds.[12]

So, then, many contemporary theologians see the need for new confessions of faith, be they of a comprehensive or of a limited nature and application. As they recognize that each confession is relative, they see the need, while the Church is still divided into denominations, for each denomination to interpret its legal standards with charity and elasticity. This sometimes takes the form of opting for a Book of Confessions as the United Presbyterian Church has done in the United States since 1967. Instead of being tied

12. This trend towards episcopacy is puzzling on several counts. It is puzzling in connection with the trend to admit a variety of *belief*, whereas from Ignatius of Antioch onwards, the episcopal system has always been valued precisely as guaranteeing unity in sound doctrine. The New Testament scholarship which supplies a New Testament precedent for a variety of doctrine also clarifies that the New Testament Church had a variety of church order and tends to speak of the trend to the threefold ministry as an "early Catholicism." So this seems to be a point where those involved in ecumenical discussions are refusing to follow the biblical scholars and are creating their church order out of an ecumenical pragmatism. Is it a case of trying to compensate for lack of theological unity by means of organizational uniformity?

only to the Westminster Confession, that Church is now tied to a tradition of theology which includes two Catholic Creeds, a Reformation Confession and Catechisms, a seventeenth-century Confession and Catechisms, and two twentieth-century Confessions. In this connection I am reminded of the much-quoted statement of E. Käsemann that "the New Testament Canon is not the ground of the unity of the Church, but rather of the diversity of the Confessions."[13]

Lessons for Evangelicals

What should a good evangelical make of this seemingly shifting sand? If he is committed, as were Rainy, Orr, and Warfield, to the inspiration and authority of the Scriptures, should he reject everything which most modern theologians appear to take for granted? Should he view the doctrine of his own denomination or favorite theologian as a healthy and sound distillation of biblical theology and ignore both the other Protestant formulations and what modern theologians are telling him about development?

There are good reasons for holding to the inspiration and authority of Scripture while, at the same time, learning from modern theologians. Since I shall propose an evangelical approach to development of doctrine in the final chapter of this book, I shall merely indicate here how evangelicals can learn from the scholars I have been summarizing.

1. Evangelicals should recognize that the unity of the New Testament (and of the whole Bible) is a unity in plurality, and that the problems involved in interpreting the Bible to create doctrine for today are real and not imaginary.[14]
2. Evangelicals should accept the humanity, relative to historical and cultural conditioning, of both the Catholic creeds and, even more so, of the Confessions of Faith of

13. E. Käsemann, *Exegetische Versuche und Besinnungen I* (Göttingen, 1960), p. 221. The essay in which the quote appears is found in his *Essays on New Testament Themes* (Naperville, IL: Allenson, 1964), pp. 95–107.
14. See further James G. Dunn, *Unity and Diversity in the New Testament* (London: SCM, 1977).

Protestantism. To recognize the humanity of doctrinal statements is not necessarily to deny that they can be or are true in what they affirm and deny.[15]

3. Evangelicals should acknowledge that all theories of homogeneous progress or development of doctrine are inadequate in the light of historical knowledge as it exists today.

4. Evangelicals should reflect on the fact that though they all profess a strong commitment to the inspiration and authority of the Bible they still represent a wide spectrum of doctrinal interpretations—e.g., baptism.

5. Evangelicals need to realize that since the theological questions being asked today are not normally the same as those asked in the sixteenth or seventeenth centuries, there is often the need, and at some times more obviously than others, for contemporary confessions of faith.[16]

Additional thought on development of doctrine should be given to that doctrine of Scripture which regards the Bible as the inerrant, infallible Word of God and which is rejected by those views previously considered. Those who hold this today do so with a tenacity which is matched only by that of the old-style Roman Catholic who clings to the Latin, Tridentine Mass. The view of the Bible referred to is usually said to be that view expounded with brilliance by B. B. Warfield and popularized in recent days by Harold Lindsell in his *Battle for the Bible* (1976). Anyone who cares to study the way in which this doctrine has emerged within evangelical Protestantism will soon realize that it has not been a simple organic growth from the teaching of Calvin and the Westminster divines. It is very much the product of different responses, in highly charged situations, to threats or supposed threats to the reliability and the trustworthiness of Scripture. At Princeton, when the Hodges and

---

15. Historical relativism can be taken too far. See the comments of R. Sturch, "Historical Relativism," *Churchman*, vol. 91 (July 1977), pp. 221ff.

16. John Stott, ed., *The Lausanne Covenant* (Minneapolis: World Wide Publications, 1975).

Warfield were developing the received, traditional doctrine of Scripture in the Reformed Churches, they were making use of a definite philosophy usually called the Scottish Common-Sense Philosophy, and they were responding to questions raised by their reading of the writings of the so-called higher critics of the Bible.[17] In fashioning their new doctrine they learned from men such as F. Turretin and L. Gaussen of Switzerland, and they rejected those common evangelical views of Scripture which are usually now called "accommodation theories" and of which Philip Doddridge, the great English Nonconformist, was an influential exponent.[18]

I am not arguing against the Warfield—Packer—Schaeffer—Montgomery view, but using it to illustrate how one major doctrine, held by many evangelicals, is the product of a specific concern for truth in a definite historical situation and, as such, has a humanity built into it. It is for the reader to decide whether the humanity is merely, as it were, the outer clothing in which the truth is stated, or is something more, affecting the very nature of the doctrine.

17. J. Rogers, ed., *Biblical Authority* (Waco, TX: Word Books, 1977), pp. 35ff.
18. Doddridge's views are found in several parts of his *Works* (10 vols., 1802–1805). They were attacked by Robert Haldane in *The Evidence and Authority of Divine Revelation* (1830) and Alexander Carson in *The Inspiration of the Scriptures* (1831). From these attacks British Evangelicalism developed a view of inspiration similar to that of the Princeton divines in America.

CHAPTER SIX

RECENT ROMAN CATHOLIC VIEWS

THE RELATION of dogma to Scripture has been a problem to which all leading Roman Catholic theologians have addressed themselves in the last three decades. This is what we would expect when we recall that doctrine which has been defined by the magisterium is regarded as infallible dogma—doctrine free from error. As in Protestantism, attention was focused in the nineteenth century on development of doctrine because of the prominence of the idea of development in philosophy and the natural sciences as well as in the new histories of doctrine. Apart from Newman, it was the theologians of the Catholic Faculty at Tübingen—J. S. Drey, J. A. Möhler, and J. E. Kuhn—who tried in the middle of the century to work out a progressive idea of development in history.[1] Since their time, further factors have transformed the question of development into a burning issue which cannot be avoided. These factors include the teaching of Anton Günther, the Jesuit Hegelian philosopher,[2] the writings of the Modernists (e.g., A. Loisy,

1. The best treatment of the Tübingen School is J. R. Geiselmann, *Die katholische Tübinger Schule. Ihre theologische Eigenart* (Herder of Freiburg, 1964).
2. For Günther see the article in the *Oxford Dictionary of the Christian Church*, F. L. Cross, ed. (New York: Oxford Univ. Press, 1974), where various studies are cited.

M. Blondel, G. Tyrrell, and F. von Hügel)[3] at the turn of the century, and the dogmatic definition in 1950 of the Bodily Assumption of Mary.[4] The latter and that of the Immaculate Conception punctuate the problem, for they are doctrines which are not required by Scripture and are not the only possible doctrines that can harmonize with the information concerning Mary found in Scripture. The definitions provided by the Second Vatican Council (1962–65) have not only given theologians a greater liberty to pursue answers to this problem, but they have also made the problem more difficult by increasing the options available to the theologian.

Before Newman, Möhler, and the Modernists introduced ideas of doctrinal progress based on evolutionary models, the way used by theologians to illustrate the relationship of dogma to the teaching of the Bible was by means of logic. That is, any new dogmatic statement given to the Church by the Pope as the true Faith had been gained by logical deduction from revealed statements in Scripture by means of the syllogism. For example,

The Bible teaches that God was in Christ (a revealed premise).

The Bible teaches that Christ was a true man (a revealed premise).

therefore the certain deduction is:

Christ is both God and Man, having two natures.

This reasoning worked, or appeared to work, for the dogma of one Christ with two natures (the definition of Chalcedon) but it seems to us today to have been less certain in other areas of doctrine. For example,

The apostle Peter was the first Vicar of Christ (based on Matthew 16:18).

The apostle Peter was the first Bishop of Rome (based on "facts" of history).

Therefore,

3. See A. R. Vidler, *A Variety of Catholic Modernists* (New York: Cambridge Univ. Press, 1970).
4. For further details see the article by H. F. David, ed., in *The Catholic Dictionary of Theology*, vol. 1 (Nashville: Nelson, 1962).

The successors of Peter in Rome are also Vicars of Christ.

Nevertheless, this belief that dogma was merely the logical development or clarification of the revealed, propositional truths of Scripture was rarely questioned from the time of the medieval scholastics until the early decades of the nineteenth century.[5] The First Vatican Council (1869–70) taught the permanence of the meaning of dogma, and the official reaction of the hierarchy to modernism until after 1950 was to assert the immutability of dogma in uncompromising terms. And, even in this century, sophisticated logical theories of the formation of dogma have been produced by three able theologians—R. M. Schultes, F. Marin-Sola, and M. Tuyaerts.[6]

Critics of the logical type of theory claim (in my view rightly) that its exponents confuse the psychological and the logical aspects of reasoning. They identify the structure of the logical connections in a syllogism with discursive thought as a factual, psychological activity, and regard the definition of the logical structure of this as the definition of the discursive reasoning itself. One writer states that:

> From the psychological point of view, discursive thought is merely the totality of experiential knowledge—in other words, it is continuously growing experience, controlled, not by subjective factors, but by the object itself that becomes more and more completely contained in explicit knowledge. Thus discursive reasoning is a gradually increasing appropriation and taking possession of something that was already previously present in the total consciousness, but not yet an explicit possession. The syllogism is, therefore, only meaningful when it is used as an element of experiential knowledge, since the concept can only grasp reality as an element of experience. Logical thought only controls the explicit aspect of thought. In expressly conceptual thought, which assumes

5. O. Chadwick, *From Bousset to Newman* (London: Cambridge Univ. Press, 1957), illustrates how it worked in the theology of the great Bousset.
6. Schultes, *Introductio in historiam dogmatum* (Paris, 1922); Marin-Sola, *L'Evolution, homogène du Dogme catholique* (Fribourg, 1924); and Tuyaerts, *L'Evolution du dogme* (Louvain, 1919).

experiential knowledge, it is the noetic structure of experience that is revealed and critically tested.[7]

Furthermore, as the teaching on Scripture provided by Vatican II indicates, the Bible is no longer seen by theologians as a source-book of revealed propositions and axioms.

Having set the context for understanding recent Roman Catholic approaches to the development of doctrine, I shall now look at the contributions of three men who have written on this topic.

Karl Rahner (b. 1904)

Rahner is well known to Protestants through his editing of *Sacramentum Mundi* (6 vols., 1968–70) and his volumes of *Theological Investigations,* which have now reached fourteen in English translation. He combines intellectual modesty with audacity and so usually stimulates his readers or hearers to reflect again on that which they believed they had already sorted out and clarified.[8] Here I shall use volumes one and four of the *Theological Investigations,* published in 1961 and 1966 respectively, for they include discussions on development of dogma.

He recalls that Roman Catholic theologians have been called upon in recent years, particularly by the neo-orthodox theologians of the school of Barth and Brunner, to state what foundation in Scripture there is for the Marian dogma which has been created in recent times. This request, he admits, is a reasonable one and it points to the complex problem of development which admits of no simple solution. It is a difficult problem:

> ... because it ultimately reaches down to the obscure depths of a general ontology of being and becoming, of the persistence of identity in change—and also comprises the general metaphysics of knowledge and mind, which frames the same questions in searching for truth, with regard to its identity and real historical development. (IV, p. 5)

7. E. Schillebeeckx, *Revelation and Theology* (New York: Sheed & Ward, 1967), p. 74.
8. For a study of his theology see L. Roberts, *The Achievement of Karl Rahner* (New York: Herder & Herder, 1967).

So it is not surprising that he readily admits that there can be no "law of development":

> The *perfected* law of dogmatic development may only be laid down when the whole, unique process has reached its term. And because it is a genuinely historical process, under the impulse of the Spirit of God, who never makes himself accessible without remainder to laws which can be grasped by human minds, it is never just the working out of a formula and an all-embracing law. (I, p. 41)

But this does not mean that nothing rational can be said of dogmatic development. Rahner himself says quite a lot.

He begins by claiming that there is a development of doctrine within the New Testament, as the apostles develop the teaching of Jesus:

> St. Paul's doctrine . . . of the sacrificial character of the cross of Christ, of Christ as the second Adam, of original sin, many sayings about eschatology etc., much of the Johannine theology etc., are theological developments from a few very simple assertions of Jesus about the mystery of his person, and from the experience of his resurrection. (IV, p. 7)

This development of dogma within Scripture is, for Rahner, the "authenticated exemplary instance for the development of dogma in general," an example which he sees as obligatory for all theologians who accept the authority of Holy Scripture.

Here I must introduce his analogy of a young man being "head over heels" in love with a young woman. This love may have presuppositions of a psychological and physiological kind which are totally unknown to him. What he knows is the experience of being in love and he knows more about his love than he can state. His love-letters do not even convey what his heart and mind feels. If he is an intelligent person and has at his disposal an adequate stock of ideas he can probably, over a period of time and from a variety of angles, state what he knows about his love. His final statements (propositions) would be statements of what he already knows but could not previously adequately express at an earlier stage in his love. Between the inner knowledge of love and the expression of this experience in propositional statements, there is no logical connection. Reflexive, articulated consciousness of an original, unreflective, conscious possession of a reality is, therefore, a possible if not common experience in the life of human beings.

For the understanding of the development of dogma both inside and outside the Canon of the New Testament, Rahner finds this analogy helpful. He holds that the apostles had a greater experience of God in Christ than ever they could put into words and so their theological expressions were "uttered out of the entirety of this living conscious contact with the incarnate God" (I, p. 66). Likewise, the experience of God in the Church is greater than words can express. There is certainly a difference between the postapostolic and the apostolic experience of the incarnate God; the former is only possible because of the latter, because experience of God comes today through the apostolic word and the same Spirit given originally to the apostles. Yet, accepting these qualifications, it can be said there is the same connection between what is implicit as a living possession of the whole truth in an unreflective but conscious way, and what is always only partially explicit in propositions. The Church, in communion with God the Father, Son, and Holy Spirit, continually strives in history towards a better articulation of its experience, and this striving results in the development of dogma. Each fresh attempt is new and yet at the same time is related to the former attempts because every attempt at any time and in any place is but a further, perhaps deeper, penetration of the original, global experience of the apostles.

For any adequate theory of this type of dogmatic development, Rahner argues that there are three *a priori* rules which cannot be overlooked. The first is that this development is a unique process which cannot be adequately comprehended or captured by formal laws. The history of dogmas is full of surprises, and the way in which one of these emerged is not the same as the way others emerged, or will emerge. The second is that the revelation in Christ is the final, unsurpassable revelation, which was closed with the end of the apostolic generation. Such a revelation, he argues, "implies a believing Church which, as a whole, cannot fall away from the faith, though nothing can be said about individuals as such" (IV, p. 9). The third is that the development of dogma is necessarily carried along, in an ultimately indissoluble way, by all those elements which are constitutive of revelation and of the self-developing dogma. The first element is the presence of God. Rahner refers here to that dimension in the apostolic and post-apostolic Church which is supernatural. The Holy Spirit is in the Church. The grace of God through Christ by the Holy Spirit is a reality which cannot be ignored, not even in the doctrinal work of the Church. Second, there is the magisterium of the Church. At the beginning the teaching of the apostles was authoritative. After their time, theologians arrive at the best expression of the Faith and this is submitted to the Church through the Pope and the college of bishops for their approval. Third, there is the concept and the word. Revelation, recorded in Scripture, is given in concepts and words which are rooted in specific cultures. The development of doctrine must also take place through concepts and words from other cultures. Fourth, there is tradition. The apostolic Church passed on to later generations the Old Testament and its own new writings, and all these books, as the Bible, are passed on within the life of the Church from one generation to the next. As the Bible is passed on, so also is an interpretation of it. This tradition should tend towards an ever clearer view of the "mystery of the Gospel." Finally, there is "the acknowledged presence of dogma, as dogma, as revealed by God." Before they saw the risen Lord and received his Spirit, the apostles had only a minimal understanding of the mystery of the incarnate God. After Pentecost they began to articulate their experience of God in Christ. So new doctrine emerged and the apostles were conscious that they were creating new doctrine (e.g., Paul's doctrine of Jesus as universal Lord). Likewise in the Church, when a new dogma is proclaimed as being a truth which God has revealed, there enters into the explicit consciousness of the whole Church this particular truth. A new dimension of understanding the mystery of the Faith is added to the understanding already there.

What I have just summarized was written before Vatican II. Since then Rahner has been even more impressed by the irreducible pluralism of human languages, thought-forms, and worldviews. In an article in *Concilium* (1969) on "Pluralism in Theology" he emphasizes that there is no longer, not even in Europe, a common philosophy and theology in which theologians can work. Thus, he does not speak only of the cessation of the old type of dogmatic developments (e.g., Mariology), but also claims that "we may well have to assume that in the future the magisterium will not be able to formulate new emphatic doctrinal pronouncements." He finds it impossible to immunize the concepts and words used in doctrinal statements (e.g., in *Humani Generis* and *Mysterium Fidei*) from problems of interpretation and historical discontinuity. So, after having begun as a young man with views of homogeneous development of doctrine, he has now, as an old man, adopted views of development of doctrine which emphasize discontinuity rather than continuity, and the episodic rather than the evolutionary.

Edward Schillebeeckx (b. 1914)

Schillebeeckx, the acknowledged leader of Roman Catholic theologians in the Netherlands, established his reputation in Britain and America with his book *Christ the Sacrament* (1963). Since then he has published two collections of essays called "Theological Soundings"; the first is *Revelation and Theology* (1967) and the second is *Concept of Truth and Theological Renewal* (1968). To an extent not found in Rahner, Schillebeeckx emphasizes that the study of the development of dogma must grow out of the study of the development of tradition. By this means he hopes to keep the perspective of the handing on of the revelation from God in the whole Church.

He begins with the insistence that revelation is not only

revelation-in-word but also revelation-in-reality. An illustration will help to clarify his meaning. What is passed on in the life of the Church in connection with the Eucharist is both a doctrine and the spiritual reality of the celebration. The two are closely connected but different. At the service of worship the Christian comes into contact with the revelation-in-word as well as the saving grace and presence of Christ—the revelation-in-reality. Now this contact with and benefit from the presence of Christ is only possible by the inner illumination of the Spirit, called by Aquinas the *lumen fidei*—"light of faith."

> This light of faith enables me to grasp more in the mystery of revelation than is said about it in conceptual terms and than history tells us about it. The material objects of faith enter our conscious minds by way of the Church's proclamation of the word (*fides ex auditu*—or 'faith by learning and listening') and the historical saving fact of the living Church herself. We do not, however, come into contact with the formal object of faith in this way, but in a purely supernatural way, through the inner impulse of the grace of faith or light of faith. (*Revelation and Theology*, p. 83)

Therefore, we have the objective revelation written in Scripture, the reality of the God who revealed himself, and the inner light of faith which recognizes and responds to the revelation and the reality of God. Development of doctrine occurs in the sphere of the *determinatio fidei*—the transition from the preliminary, implicit stage to explicit knowledge. So Schillebeeckx sees the continuity of the faith of the church in the light of faith possessed by the faithful at all times, and, since the development of doctrine is the attempt to put this implicit faith into an explicit verbal form, then development of doctrine also has its ultimate meaning in the inner work of the Holy Spirit.

He holds that whenever there is a faithful external presentation of the content of the implicit faith of the whole Church, then that presentation cannot be wrong. Individuals or groups of individuals who attempt to explain their faith will probably err because their explanation takes in factors other than the reality of the inner faith itself; it becomes conditioned by too many aspects of human life in a given situation. True development of dogma is only possible in the whole Church.

> Although it is in the first place deeply influenced by strongly religious personalities, the growth of the church's faith is still a communal work. The development, according to which dogma grows from an implicit preliminary phase to the explicit stage is a very slow process of maturation in the bosom of the Church, within which all kinds of influence throw light on each other—within which opinions, conjectures and theological considerations are offered to the community and exposed to the reaction of its members. This is a constant process of friction and purification in which all members of the church community play a part. (*Revelation and Theology*, pp. 87–88)

Gradually, however, in and through the implicit and explicit process of development, the light of faith within the body of Christians makes itself more and more strongly felt until all the various voices converge and the firm conviction grows in the Church that a definitive statement is necessary. In this way, the faith of the universal church cannot err.

Assuming that the Church has an infallible teaching authority, Schillebeeckx sees this teaching office active in all the stages, but supremely so in the final acceptance of the doctrine and its propagation to and for the Church:

> We may therefore conclude that the converging activity of the light of faith in the community of faith of the Church, together with the Church's infallible teaching office is the single structural principle of the unchangeable character of the faith throughout all its different phases of development. The laws and factors which cause any human ideology to mature, including implicit thought and reflective reasoning, thus play an active part in the development of dogma. As such, however, they cannot make the datum of faith develop in its properly supernatural element. For this reason, they only play an instrumental part with regard to the activity of the light of faith and the teaching authority of the church. (*Revelation and Theology*, p. 91)

This instrumental human factor explains why certain dogmas were defined at a late stage in the history of the Church and why each dogma is related to a particular historical context and language.

In the later thinking of Schillebeeckx, there has emerged the idea of development by demolition. He holds that this is necessary since, within the general progress of dogma, each dogmatic formulation contains representational elements which are determined by a particular historical period and situation. These elements must be relinquished later if the essential aspects of these formulations are to be preserved. For example, in the move to a Copernican view of the universe the doctrine of the ascension of Christ was stripped of its Ptolemaic modes of expression. Naturally, before such a "demolition" can take place the Church has to be aware of the underlying images and ideas used in the statement and has to replace them with new images and ideas. Schillebeeckx has illustrated this "demolition" with reference to the Roman Catholic doctrine of marriage.[9] The traditional view of marriage, he argues, is wedded to a doctrine of natural law which few accept today. New views in our contemporary culture about the nature of man and his place in society call for a restatement of the doctrine of marriage and such aspects as the regulation of birth.

Gabriel Moran

Perhaps best known in America as a writer on the philosophy and principles of Christian education, Brother Moran has addressed himself briefly but creatively to the development of doctrine in his book *Theology of Revelation* (1966), which deserves to be better known.

His understanding of development is set in the context of his thesis that "the risen and glorified Lord is the one place where Revelation continues to happen in fullness" (p. 75). In the exalted human consciousness of Jesus Christ, God's total revelation is received and understood not only for

9. E. Schillebeeckx, "De natuurwet in verband met de katholieke huwelijksopvatting," Jaarboek 1961, *Werkgenootschap van katholieke theologen in Nederland* (Hilversum, 1963), pp. 26ff.

himself but also for his people, the body of Christ. Everything to which the Old and New Testaments witness is gathered in the glorified humanity of Jesus, the very humanity which is inseparably linked in one *prosōpon* with the deity. By and through the Holy Spirit, the exalted Lord gives to the Church both spiritual gifts and revelation. By the Spirit, the apostles received a deep understanding of that which Jesus Christ had perfectly received and understood. So they claimed to speak words which could bring people face to face with Christ (Gal. 3:1). These were in fact God's words, for they represented that perfect revelation received by Christ and given to them by him. They made clear the mystery—the content of God's self-revelation.

The mystery of the gospel is Jesus Christ; but this mystery is not that of the detective novel which, at the end of the book, ceases to be a mystery, for we know all the secrets. Neither is it that type of mystery which has no meaning. Rather, God revealed in Jesus Christ is a mystery not because there is nothing more to say of him but because there is always *more* to say. The more God's mystery was revealed to Paul by the Spirit of the exalted Lord, the more he appreciated the depth of God's wisdom (Rom. 11:33):

> The 'mystery of God' is found in Jesus Christ whose own grasp of the revealing God was certainly not in the form of doctrines about God. The incomprehensible presence of the Logos to the humanity of Jesus was the unsurpassable Revelation of God to man (John 1). This revelation was only gradually assimilated by Christ into objective and communicable knowledge as he lived the mystery of God, that is, his own existence in the world with other men. His experience could not be exhausted with human statements. Nevertheless, he could during his lifetime make true statements about God, statements which were neither false nor empty. (p. 134)

The apostles lived with Christ and were taught by him after his resurrection from the dead. Further, they received the special guidance of the Spirit throughout the time of the Church's foundation; thus, their conceptual expression of their experience of the "mystery" became more accurate. This is not to say that their first statements were false because all words spoken from within the "mystery" are true to the extent that they give insight into the "mystery." Therefore, there is a development of doctrine within the New Testament reflecting different degrees of appreciation of the "mystery of Christ": "Scripture is not a collection of revealed words and judgments from which deductions can be made. It is rather a testimony of faith to the Revelation made full in the conscious experience of Christ and his apostles" (p. 137).

Reflection on the mystery of Christ in the Church has always been mediated by the privileged testimony of the apostles. By the Spirit, and through the means of the sacred writings, the exalted Lord is sharing with the Church his understanding of God's self-revelation. In this sense, revelation is continually occurring as the Church gains deeper insights into that process which was completed in the resurrection and ascension of Jesus. Since the Spirit, who is free (John 3:8), guides the Church in her understanding and is the guarantee of continuity, theologians search in vain for a logical or deductive link in the process of development. So Moran follows Rahner in claiming that "no all-inclusive law of doctrinal development can be laid down *a priori*; the perfected law of development can be seen only at the term of the whole process" (p. 139).

The Church in history both bears the revelation and is borne by the revelation. Yet, the people of the Church must speak of God's revelation from within the language of their world. By this interaction new concepts and words are formed which help to express, in explicit statements, the revelation, known already implicitly in experience of God. Just as the human experience of Christ was necessary for the development of revelation in his earthly experience, so too the experience of peoples in different centuries is necessary for the complete and perfected reception of revelation in the Church.

What part does the hierarchy of the Church have in development? It is not to possess and hand down the revelation but rather to listen to, to guide, and to protect the faith of the whole Church in the living of revelation. God's guidance was promised to the whole people of God, and thus each and every member participates in the receiving of revelation. The continuity of the Church and her preservation from failure is ultimately the work of the Spirit. Yet, since the Church is a human society, guidance needs to find expression in a human authority structure which is not opposed to Bible or Spirit. This magisterium is not there to impose an interpretation but rather to ensure that all parts of the Church make their contribution to the development of understanding the "mystery of Christ." So the teaching office of the Church cannot be separated from the believing Church.

In defining doctrines, the purpose of the magisterium is not to disintegrate the mystery but to invite the faithful to a deeper participation in the mystery. Also, it is to protect the mystery from the "prying rationalism" of men.

> Even conciliar definitions are more in the nature of starting points or frameworks within which to live and work than of conclusions. Each of the truths reached in the Church's progress is intended to bring into greater unity the witness to a Revelation which is refracted through, but never bottled up in, human statements. The truth which the Church has taken possession of she does not then leave behind; but every ecclesial formulation, while itself remaining valid, can in principle be improved upon through reformulation. (p. 145).

As language changes so the language used by the Church must change, and even the guidance of the Spirit does not mean that the Church will never make mistakes.

* * *

It is impossible to forcast where Roman Catholic thinking on development of doctrine is heading. One thing, however, is clear. Both theologians and parish priests are now much more prepared than at any other time since the Reformation to discuss with Protestants the teaching of Scripture, the nature of dogma, and such matters as historical relativism and situationalism. Let us not miss this opportunity, for we have much to learn from some Roman Catholic writers.[10] In particular, I would like to commend

10. Cf. G. C. Berkouwer, *A Half Century of Theology* (Grand Rapids: Eerdmans 1977), chapter eight, "Concern for the Faith."

Bernard Lonergan's *Method in Theology* (1975) to my Protestant colleagues. I shall refer to another book by Lonergan in the next chapter.[11]

11. There is a helpful essay by G. A. Lindbeck, "Protestant Problems with Lonergan on Development of Dogma," in *Foundations of Theology*, P. McShane, ed. (Notre Dame, IN: Univ. of Notre Dame Press, 1971).

CHAPTER SEVEN

A CONTEMPORARY
EVANGELICAL VIEW

IN THIS CHAPTER I shall attempt to provide an evangelical view of development of doctrine. While there may be disagreement with the view expressed here, it is my hope that the discussion will at least lead to a serious consideration of the issue.

I shall take for granted that for Christians the only authoritative basis for faith and doctrine is the revelation of God of which the books of the Bible are the written, unique record. I recognize that I can be accused of beginning with a developed doctrine in order to explain the development of doctrine! In fact, I use this principle of the authority of the Bible, not as a dogma which some competent ecclesiastical body has defined, but as a deep conviction which is possible to articulate in several ways, and which the Church has possessed from the earliest times of her history. The recent bitter debates surrounding the *Battle for the Bible* indicate that even among evangelicals there is no single doctrine of Scripture. (Indeed, I doubt whether there can be a doctrine of Scripture until we can agree on the way in which the New Testament writers use the Old Testament.[1]) Secondly, I shall presume that one part of the work of the Church on earth involves the making of doctrine. Through doctrine the

1. See the studies, for example, by E. E. Ellis (1957), B. Lindars (1961), N. Lohfink (1969), R. T. France (1971), and D. L. Baker (1976).

Church instructs her members, and by doctrine the members can better worship and serve God. Also, by means of doctrine the Church can protect herself against heresy from within and attacks from without. Thirdly, I shall assume that, whatever development of doctrine exists within the Bible, such as, from the Old to the New Testament and from the Gospels to the Epistles, it has no *direct* bearing on the development of doctrine in the historical Church after the days of the apostles. As Rainy made clear, and as Oscar Cullmann agrees, the development of doctrine in the Bible is part of the unique *Heilsgeschichte* (salvation-history).[2]

The Nature of Dogma

Initially, it will be helpful to investigate the useful distinction made by Rainy between divine truth or teaching as embodied in Scripture, and doctrine as formulated by believers. In order to formulate a view of development it is certainly necessary to clarify what is an ecclesiastical doctrine or dogma, and what relation dogma has to Scripture. Because the first dogma of the Church was the deity of Jesus of Nazareth, I shall examine this in order to define dogma. I shall follow the argument of Bernard Lonergan in his *The Way to Nicea* (1976), which is a translation of the first part of his monumental treatise *De Deo Trino*, published in Rome in 1964. (In using Lonergan's analysis I do not necessarily make the high claims for the trans-cultural nature of Nicene dogma which he makes.)

The writings of the New Testament, though they certainly contain true propositions, are not just a collection of propositions, addressed only to the intellect of man. Rather, the books contain truth in ordinary language and this language makes its appeal to the whole man. So, claims Lonergan, the contents "penetrate the sensibility, fire the imagination, engage the affections, touch the heart, open the eyes, attract and impel the will of the reader." Dogmatic decrees of a Council are different: "so clearly and so accurately do

2. O. Cullmann, *Salvation in History* (New York: Harper & Row, 1967).

they declare what is true that they seem to bypass the senses, the feelings and the will to appeal only to the mind." Between the contents of Scripture and the propositions of a Church Council there is a process of synthesis by which the many sayings of Scripture are reduced to a fundamental proposition which often makes use of technical language, such as, "Jesus Christ is of the same *ousia* as the Father."

This distinction between the truth in the ordinary language of the Bible and the precise language of the creed is not unfamiliar in other areas of human experience. Take, for example, the different ways in which ordinary people and meteorologists talk about the weather. I recognize hot and cold days, windy and calm conditions, and dry and rainy periods. I talk about this (and the English seem always to talk about the weather) to my neighbors and colleagues. My friend, an expert on weather, can understand my ordinary language and generally accepts its accuracy. However, although he observes the same weather as I do, he uses a technical language and data with computer models to describe and forecast it. Until I am trained, I cannot appreciate all his technical language. Obviously there is a need in our technological society for both ordinary and technical language about the weather. Both are valid in their own spheres. Likewise biblical and credal language are valid.

To put the distinction in another way, it may be claimed, with E. Schlink, that theological statements in the Bible fall into four types—prayer, doxology, witness, and doctrine.[3] There are many examples of prayer—the prayers of Moses, Jesus, and Paul. Doxology, or praise and adoration, is also addressed to God and is the theological development of thankfulness for God's action and word. Many psalms and Ephesians 1 are examples. Witness is the response to the gospel which is addressed to others. Examples are the sermons in the Acts of the Apostles. Finally, doctrine is con-

3. See further Edmund Schlink, "The Structure of Dogmatic Statements as an Ecumenical Problem," in *The Coming Christ and the Coming Church*, trans. G. Overlack and D. B. Simmonds (Philadelphia: Fortress, 1967), pp. 16–84. Perhaps the category of history should make a fifth type (John 1:14; Acts 2:4, etc.).

cerned with the gospel and its interpretation. Examples are parts of John's Gospel and of Paul's epistles to Galatia and Rome. These four types of theological statement are combined in a credal or dogmatic statement of the Church. So we may say that if the Church dogma loses, for example, the doxological dimension, it is hardly being true to Scripture.

Dogmatic development as seen at Nicea, claims Lonergan, has four main aspects—an objective, a subjective, an evaluative, and a hermeneutical. The objective aspect has two separate elements or transitions. First, there is the transition from one literary genre to another. The Scriptures are addressed to the whole person in common sense language while the decree or dogma aims only at enlightening the intellect through precise expressions. Secondly, there is a transition from a complexity of truths to a single truth. In the Bible truths are intertwined with each other and with practical exhortation, whereas in a dogma attention is focused on one truth in isolation.

Corresponding to the objective is the subjective aspect of development. Lonergan has described this in detail in *Insight: A Study of Human Understanding* (1957). It involves a transition from undifferentiated common sense, which is the normal type of experience for most people most of the time, to the intellectual pattern of experience. This transition from understanding a reality vaguely, generally, and imprecisely (as far as scientific criteria are concerned) to understanding it precisely and particularly does not occur overnight, for there is a slow learning process which demands serious effort. I find, for example, in teaching the doctrine of the Trinity, whether to ordinands or to lay leaders, that it takes them so much time and mental energy to grasp the concepts involved that they often confess to being mentally exhausted at the end! Hence, to achieve a clear idea of what the orthodox doctrine of the Trinity is stating is to enter into the region of precise conceptual thinking, and few of us enter this region in normal religious activity.

The evaluative aspect relates to that characteristic of thinking engaged in by human beings, who not only act but also pause to reflect upon and pass judgments on their actions. The more sophisticated the civilization, the more time some people have to reflect and evaluate. Thus, in creating dogma in the civilized Roman Empire, the theologians of the Church, with their developed intellectual ability, reflected upon their faith and worship and upon revelation. Then they made an evaluation of the evidence in order to produce their propositions concerning what they held to be the truth.

Finally, there is the hermeneutical aspect. The human mind is not equally open to all ideas as if it were a busy street where all may come and go. Whatever is received by the mind is received "after the manner of the receiver." That is, in studying something, the mind makes a selection of the many aspects it could take in and then structures and imposes a unity on the selection. The Christians who faced the question, "What is the truth concerning the relation of Jesus of Nazareth to God the Father?" were Greeks, and made their selection and imposed their unity in a way different from what, for example, a group of Chinese Christian theologians would have done.

These four aspects belong together. The objective aspect of dogmatic development presupposes the ability to think conceptually. The evaluative and hermeneutical are intimately related, for whatever is presented to the mind for consideration is received by the mind within the perimeters of its basic assumptions and convictions (which are, of course, related to specific languages and cultures). Those who have taught a class, or been members of a seminar, with Europeans, Asians, and Africans will easily understand this.

Lonergan makes two further important observations. First, while there occurred in the early ecumenical councils a development in Trinitarian and Christological doctrine, there also emerged in the Church the very notion of dogma. Technically speaking, there was no dogma before the Council of Nicea. Since then there has been much dogma! Before Nicea there were different theologies and varied presentations of the God of revelation in the one Church. After Nicea there was an official doctrine of the relation of Jesus Christ to God the Father. The second point is that the development of doctrine from the Scriptures to the Creed of Nicea is not from obscurity to clarity, but from one kind of clarity to another. What Matthew, Mark, Luke, and John wrote about Jesus was not obscure but clear; yet, their clear teaching acquired a new kind of clarity through the dogma of Nicea. Most Christians live their lives by the clarity of the Scriptures, and those Christians with active intellectual powers live by both the clarity of Scripture and the clarity of dogma.

Before moving on to further illustrations of dogma, I would like to point out that historical situationalism is necessarily involved in the four aspects of development. This is especially obvious in the evaluative and hermeneutical aspects, for the people who are involved in these aspects of development belong to specific cultures and intellectual traditions. Therefore, ecclesiastical doctrine is always expressed in words and concepts that are grounded in a particular culture.

The dogma of the Trinity found in the extended Nicene Creed approved by the Council of Constantinople (381), and the dogma of Christ as One Person with Two Natures produced by the Council of Chalcedon (451), may claim to be precise summaries of that to which all Scripture points. They do not represent merely a Pauline or Johannine viewpoint but a comprehensive viewpoint—a synthesis. There are, however, later doctrines which either represent a major biblical viewpoint or are the result of the devotional life of a part of the Church.

An example of a doctrine representing *one* major New Testament presentation is that of justification by faith, which is largely Pauline. I quote from the Belgic Confession (1561):

ARTICLE XXII
Of Our Justification Through Faith in Jesus Christ

We believe that, to attain the true knowledge of this great mystery, the Holy Ghost kindleth in our hearts an upright faith, which embraces Jesus Christ with all his merits, appropriates him, and seeks nothing more besides him. For it must needs follow, either that all things which are requisite to our salvation are not in Jesus Christ, or if all things are in him, that then those who possess Jesus Christ through faith have complete salvation in Him. Therefore, for any to assert that Christ is not sufficient, but that something more is required besides him, would be too gross a blasphemy; for hence it would follow that Christ was but half a Saviour. Therefore we justly say with Paul, that we are justified by faith alone, or by faith without works. However, to speak more clearly, we do not mean that faith itself justifies us, for it is only an instrument with which we embrace Christ our Righteousness. But Jesus Christ, imputing to us all his merits, and so many holy works, which he hath done for us and in our stead, is our Righteousness. And faith is an instrument that keeps us in communion with him in all his benefits, which, when they become ours, are more than sufficient to acquit us of our sins.

If we examine the proof-texts supplied in the footnotes we find that there are twenty-seven, of which twenty are from the writings of Paul, two from the Psalms (51:13 and 32:1–2), three from Jeremiah (23:6 twice and 31:10), one from 1 Peter (1:4–5), one from Matthew (1:21), and one from Acts (4:12). The Old Testament texts can be discounted since Paul quotes them, and so we are left with three from non-Pauline material—and these, we can fairly say, are interpreted by means of Paul's teaching.

The example of a doctrine being a rationale for the deep-rooted devotional life of part of the Church (Roman Catholicism) is provided by the Assumption of the Blessed Virgin Mary, a dogma promulgated by the Pope in 1950 in the document *Munificentissimus Deus*. This dogma asserts that, having completed her earthly life, the blessed Virgin Mary was assumed, body and soul, into the heavenly glory without experiencing death. Now, as all educated Roman Catholics admit, there is obviously no *direct* biblical evidence for this doctrine (and for this reason I would reject it). Yet, it represents a belief which has grown in the Church over the centuries and which, it is held, is not contrary to any biblical teaching.

While the four aspects of doctrine can be seen in the creation of the Protestant doctrine of justification, they are perhaps less obvious in the Roman doctrine of the Assumption of Mary. The reason for this is that, with the latter, the transition is not only from the biblical but also from the liturgical data to the precise theological statement of 1950. Therefore, the process of synthesis is different.

Having described the nature of conciliar or confessional doctrine, I must point out that it is possible to understand doctrine in a wider sense. Jaroslav Pelikan gives the following helpful definition: "Christian doctrine is what the Church believes, teaches, and confesses on the basis of the Word of God."[4] He formulated this definition in order to challenge Harnack's restrictive definition of doctrine and to emphasize that the ecclesiastical doctrine in creeds and decrees cannot be isolated from other expressions of doctrine in such activities as preaching, teaching, exegesis, liturgy, and spirituality. In the life of the churches, official doctrine is always found in a larger context of doctrine, which has never been precisely stated in a credal form. Recently, for example, certain assumptions concerning the work and presence of the Spirit in the Church have been widespread, but they have not been stated as official doctrine. Regarding development, we are primarily concerned with official doctrine, but we recognize that before doctrines become credal they often are imprecisely known by the Church.

A further comment is necessary. We look for orthodoxy in a church in the ordinary language of worship, prayer, preaching, witness, and evangelism. Dogmas or ecclesiastical doctrines are second-level statements which are meant to guide the use of ordinary language in the congregation. Dogmas should not be preached as a substitute for expounding the Scriptures to the people; neither should they become the content of piety and serve as a warrant, as in the case of the Holy Trinity, for praying equally to all three members of the Trinity. The normal pattern of Scripture is to pray to the Father, through the Son, and in the power of the Spirit. Since

4. J. Pelikan, *Historical Theology* (Philadelphia: Westminster, 1971), pp. 95–96.

it is addressed primarily to the intellect, the language of dogma is intended to guide the minds of Christians so that what they say in ordinary, common sense language is a faithful expression of the Christian understanding of God.

Development of Doctrine

Obviously, we need a way of understanding development which does justice to the unique place of Scripture, to the reality of the human society (the Church) in which the Bible is studied, to the historical situations in which Christian minds form doctrine, and to the explication of doctrine in precise intellectual terms. As my basic heuristic model, I shall use the model of doing normal science proposed by Thomas Kuhn in *The Structure of Scientific Revolutions* (2nd ed., 1970).[5]

Supporting this basic model I offer two further models. First, a model of the Church taken from 1 Timothy 3:15. Here Paul speaks of the Church of the living God as "the pillar and bulwark of the truth." This highlights the fact that one of the major tasks of the Church is to teach and defend the truth as it is in Jesus Christ. Second, to highlight the historical situations in which doctrine emerges, I shall use the model of the structured with the constituent elements, which I explained in Chapter Five.

Kuhn argues that what he calls paradigms dominate normal science. Every group of scientists (biologists, physicists, etc.) works with a cluster of broad conceptual and methodological presuppositions which are embodied in the standard examples through which the student learns the dominant theories of the particular discipline or field. A

---

5. I found I. G. Barbour, *Myths, Models, and Paradigms* (New York: Harper & Row, 1974), chapters six and seven, helpful in understanding Kuhn's book. In adopting this model I follow the suggestion and part of the exposition made by Paul Helm in an unpublished paper written for the Latimer House Study Group on Tradition in 1972. A similar suggestion was made to me in 1977 at a seminar by members of the Department of Religion and Philosophy, Western Kentucky University.

well-known example of a paradigm is Newton's work in mechanics which implicitly defined for a specific body of scientists the type of questions which could be asked, the types of explanations which could be sought, and the types of solutions which were acceptable. Thus, accepted examples of scientific practice—examples which include law, coherent theory, application, and instrumentation—provide models from which spring particular traditions of scientific research. Normal science, then, is the work done within the paradigm which defines a coherent research tradition. A shared paradigm is that which creates a scientific community with its basic assumptions and means of communication (conferences, journals, etc.). When the time comes for a radical change, as from Aristotelian to Newtonian physics, then there is a paradigm change—a revolution—after which normal science operates in a different but consistent way. Within whatever paradigm a community of scientists works, it is from that paradigm that they both view reality and form criteria by which to decide what solutions are acceptable. In addition, a community usually has a metaphysical or ontological commitment. This can be seen in the use of Newtonian mechanics: scientists understood its categories as indicative of the constituents of the universe. It can be seen also in the philosophical use of the theory of evolution.

Hence, it can be claimed that there are four stages in scientific activity: 1) observations; 2) theories and theoretical models; 3) research traditions or research programs built up over a period of time and embodied in key examples known as "exemplars"; and 4) metaphysical assumptions about the nature of entities in the world. It may be argued that the Bible contains all four elements in the common sense mode, including the realism which is metaphysical assumption. This is one way to use the model; however, for our purposes I want to discount the fourth stage and use only the first three. (I do not minimize the different philosophical assumptions of different civilizations, cultures, and centuries, but to discuss this problem here would be peripheral to the main thrust of my argument.)[6] Thus, I suggest that stages one and two correspond to the work of the biblical writers (especially those of the New Testament), and stages three and four correspond to the work of the Church theologians throughout history who work from stage two.

In the Bible we have the first and the authoritative exposition and interpretation of the revelation of God, particularly revelation in the person of Jesus Christ. For the Christian reading the Bible there are no bare facts; rather, there is a message which is an interpretation of the facts. For example, we know that Christ died and was resurrected from death; yet, according to Paul, "Christ died for our sins and 'rose for our justification.'" In fact, there is not one interpretation but a cluster of interpretations, all of which, like the colors of the rainbow, belong together. Matthean or Pauline theology can stand alone as a valid interpretation of the observed "fact," the life of Jesus of Nazareth; but the total message is provided by the insights of all the interpretations. It is this total presentation of God's message in the New Testament which provides, in Kuhn's phrase, the basic paradigm (the basic truth in common sense language).

Developing doctrine is the equivalent of doing normal science—stage three. The apostolic writings are the paradigm, and the Church attempts first to understand and then to teach the message of the paradigm. Those theologies which reject the authority of the apostolic message are excluded. Only theology done within the paradigm tradition is acceptable, and there can be no change of paradigm. Development of doctrine involves the Church in careful exegesis of the texts and then the choice of the best available concepts and words within a specific cultural situation as the means of conveying God's message for that time and place. Such a growth in understanding and expressing the

6. I understand that Dr. Kraft of the School of World Mission at Fuller Seminary is soon to publish a book on doing theology from a cross-cultural perspective. Also the new journal, *Gospel in Context* (Abingdon: Partnership in Mission), is facing this problem.

meaning of the texts is basically intellectual and theological. Thus, it is not to be equated or confused with either Christian social or evangelistic activity on the one hand or growth of knowledge of such things as social customs in biblical times on the other.

A variety of factors may contribute to the progress in understanding, such as the teaching of heretics (e.g., Arius and Pelagius), scientific discovery (e.g., by Copernicus and Galileo), theological controversy (e.g., concerning the person of Christ), and other factors, including social change. To understand the biblical paradigm, knowing what these factors are is not important (although to the historian they are very important). Also, by general consent, this development of intellectual understanding and expression is embodied in certain key "exemplars," of which two would be the doctrine of the Trinity found in the Nicene Creed and the doctrine of salvation by grace through faith found in all the Confessions of the Reformation Churches.

However, since the development of doctrine is the human and therefore imperfect elaboration of the paradigm in different historical and cultural contexts, it would be foolish to claim that all ecclesiastical doctrine represents the best possible understanding of the paradigm, just as it would be foolish to expect that all the explanations of his research provided by a young doctoral candidate in physics are beyond improvement.

Are there any criteria by which we can decide whether any given doctrine is a valid development within the paradigm tradition? Stated another way, if doing normal theology is working from and within the unique presentation of Christ provided by the apostles, and also carefully taking note of the "exemplars" (which means, I think, reading the message of God as having a Trinitarian structure to it), is there any way of deciding when this theological "research tradition" or "research program" has been genuinely developed or extended? Although I cannot recommend either James Orr's "immanent law" or John Henry Newman's infallible Pope, I believe that there are several criteria by which we can judge whether a doctrine formulated by the Church, or part of it, contains a faithful understanding and expression of the message of God in Scripture.

The first of the criteria is that *the new doctrine must positively cohere with (that is, be entailed by, not merely consistent with) what is already believed at other points.*[7] This criterion rules out the doctrine of the Bodily Assumption of Mary, for while this belief is not inconsistent with Scripture it is not required by it. The criterion also rules out a doctrine of salvation by works, for the principle that God alone gives salvation is basic to the whole New Testament and to the "exemplar" of the Holy Trinity. On the other hand, the general doctrine that there will be a judgment of the world by God at the end of the age is acceptable, for it is both required by Scripture and consistent with the Trinitarian view of God.

Bearing in mind that God's message in the New Testament is presented in several interpretations—Lucan, Pauline, and so forth—a second criterion must be that *a doctrine based on one of these major interpretations is acceptable as long as it is presented in such a way so as not to deny but rather to complement the teaching of other major interpretations.* The Protestant doctrine of justification by faith is pre-eminently based upon the Pauline interpretation of Christ, but it is acceptable in the Church if it does not deny the teaching of James and is not inconsistent with, for example, the Johannine presentation of salvation in Christ. (It is possible, and Lutherans have done it and continue to do it, to interpret the whole New Testament through Pauline eyes; on the other hand, and the Orthodox tradition appears to do this, it is possible to do the same with certain Johannine motifs!) The application of this criterion should mean that it is possible to have complementary doctrines in the Church which are not mutually exclusive. Such complementary teaching, which would form a cluster of doctrines, would not, however, represent opposite sides in the great controversies, e.g., regarding free-will and predestination; rather,

7. This criterion is the suggestion of P. Helm. The fifth and sixth come from J. I. Packer and the others are my own.

they would be developments of Pauline, Johannine, and Lucan teaching on salvation, the sacraments (ordinances), and the person and work of Christ. This way of looking at the making of doctrine, though contrary to evangelical tradition, does have possibilities for true ecumenical advance. And I would add that, in the difficult area of eschatology, the doctrine of the millennium built upon exegesis of John's Revelation would only become Church doctrine if it fitted in with the teaching of other books in the New Testament.

A third criterion is that *doctrine is only valid if it does justice to the fourfold nature of biblical theological statements—prayer, doxology, witness, and teaching.* More precisely, the ecclesiastical doctrine must not deny any of these aspects even if all four are not immediately obvious. For example, if the Church is to hold a doctrine of predestination as part of its confession that God alone is the author of salvation, then that doctrine must not exclude the doxological and prayer aspects. If the presentation of the ecclesiastical doctrine is such that it encourages speculation into God's eternal thoughts instead of worship of his name, then it is not acceptable. Much the same can be said about eschatology—if any doctrine encourages speculation as to the exact time of the end and of the possible events connected with the end, then it is unacceptable, for its role should be to encourage us "to watch and pray," to witness and to evangelize. Also, this criterion requires us to remember that ecclesiastical doctrine is meant to edify the people of God and make them better practicing Christians.

A fourth criterion is that *we should not use any supposed "exemplar" which, being the mere creation of a small part of the Church or of several people, has not found general acceptance among believing theologians.* Examples of this are such systematic interpretations of the Bible as dispensationalism and federalism (federal theology). The former was invented by J. N. Darby about 1830, and the latter by Calvinist thinkers in the seventeenth century. For many Protestant Christians, dispensationalism or federalism has become an "exemplar" more important than the "exemplar" of the Trinity, and thus it seriously affects the way in which the Scriptures are read and understood. While the dogma of the Trinity may be said to be required by the totality of the message of the Bible, the same cannot be said either of dispensationalism or federalism.

A fifth criterion is that *any valid, developed doctrine of the Church will serve to focus both the meaning and the implication of Scripture.* An obvious example is the doctrine of the Trinity and the host of passages in which the Father, Son, and Holy Spirit are named together (e.g., Matt. 28:19; 2 Thess. 2:13–14; 2 Cor. 13:14, etc.), or in which the Father and Son are mentioned, as in Christ's statement, "I and the Father are one." A further obvious example is how Christological doctrine is used in focusing the meaning of passages in which Jesus Christ is central (e.g., Phil. 2:5–11; Heb. 1:1–3, etc.). The same cannot be said of the doctrine that Christians receive the Spirit only after conversion when they are baptized in the Spirit (i.e., the older Pentecostalist teaching).

A sixth criterion is that *a developed doctrine should clarify the unity of God's revealed will, as it is portrayed in one of the "theologies of the Bible" or as it is portrayed in the total Bible.* In developed doctrine based on Paul's teaching, justification by faith does clarify God's will; that is, how God is able to remain just and still account as righteous those who are sinners. The doctrine of the Trinity likewise illustrates a deep unity between the God of Israel and the God and Father of Jesus Christ.

It is important to recognize that these criteria are for evaluating the development of doctrine as it has emerged or as it will emerge. They are not primarily intended to judge between competitive confessions of faith or between competitive systematic theologies. My criteria possibly could invalidate as total presentations some of these Confessions and books on dogmatics. In addition, these criteria do not directly help us decide what is the best form, organization, or polity for the local, national, or international church. In this area we have to look at the established tradition of the church.

Whether we like it or not we are all clothed in unsheddable cultural skins, and we must seek to understand the history of the Church, the emergence of doctrine, and the nature of dogmatic statements as people of the 1970s. I fully recognize that Kuhn's basic model used here for understanding the development of doctrine would not have been meaningful to students in the Victorian period. Obviously, their view of science was different from ours. Nevertheless, I hope that it does help modern students to see what is involved in development relative to the discussion of historical and philosophical issues.

Dogma, Divine Providence, and the Holy Spirit

Christians believe that God guides the individual as well as the visible Church. God's rule over Israel and his guidance of its people is a major theme of the Old Testament. Since the Holy Spirit was given to the Church (Acts 2) the Church has increasingly become a people of many races, lands, and cultures. Thus, the relation of the history of the Church to the history of the nations of the world is exceedingly complex. We trust and believe that Christ is Lord of history and Lord of the Church, yet at the same time we confess that we are unable precisely to plot or describe this rule. It was much easier, we often say, to plot the guidance of God when all God's people were in one nation.

Yet, one area among others where it is reasonable to expect the guidance of Christ through his Spirit is in the formation of doctrines, particularly if God knows (when we do not) the far-reaching consequences of the adoption of one dogma or another. Thus, I concur with the belief of a majority of Christians that God guided the early Church in the making of the foundational dogmas of the Trinity and the person of Christ. This is not to deny that these doctrines are integrally related to their historical situation in reference to concepts and language; but, properly understood, they are accurate statements addressed to our intellects and, therefore, though they can possibly be improved, they can never be denied. But what can be said of the other conciliar doctrines emerging in the Church of this period—on Church, ministry, and sacraments, for example? What can be learned from the doctrinal achievements of the great theologians of the Church from the fifth to the fifteenth century—Augustine, John of Damascus, Anselm, Aquinas, and others? And how are the dogmatic decrees of the various Church councils which met in East and West from the Council of Chalcedon (451) to the Council of Trent (1545–1563) evaluated? For example, the Fourth Lateran Council (1215) provided an official Western definition of how the Church was to understand the presence of Christ in the Eucharist, using the word "transubstantiation." Regarding these questions, my Protestant instincts tell me that, while I may look for the influence of the Holy Spirit in the thinking and writing of some of the theologians of the Middle Ages, I cannot believe that the Holy Spirit guided the Church to formulate all the dogma and rules which the Councils produced. Thus, while there was true, experiential knowledge and love of God in the Church, and while there was an orthodoxy based on the great dogma of the Trinity and the person of Christ, I suspect that the Holy Spirit had little to do with many of the doctrinal formulations concerning such subjects as sacraments, priesthood, and purgatory. They were merely *human* formulations in which, to use a previous model, the constituent elements had partially or wholly eclipsed the structured elements.

At the time of the Reformation, there was a tremendous movement of the Spirit leading the Church back to the Scriptures and to the gospel of Christ. This spiritual dynamic gave a clearer doctrinal understanding in the Church, which is captured by the early Confessions of Faith of this period. Regrettably, what could have been a total renewal of the Western Church turned out to be the invigoration of segments of that Church, and these segments created traditions which led them apart from the others. Thus, the doctrinal formulations of the Roman Catholics at Trent and the Protestants in the later Confessions (e.g., Belgic, Second Helvetic, etc.) were produced with the intent of stating not only what is true on the basis of Scripture, but also what is true in opposition to other views.

Finally, certain aspects of the present evangelical scene (e.g., the Lausanne Covenant) and ecumenical movement (e.g., the doctrinal agreements reached by the Roman and Anglican Commission) can be seen as reponses to the promptings of the Holy Spirit, who is working to produce a meaningful unity among God's people today. There will be no formation of dogma which possesses the quality of Nicene dogma, until it is created by a truly ecumenical council. Perhaps in the Third World, where the Spirit appears to be working powerfully in extending the Church, there will arise a generation of theologians who will produce doctrine for their own Churches and also give help, directly or indirectly, to the Church in the western hemisphere. We may be able to arrive at the point where we can assert that the unity of dogmatic statements need not consist in the acceptance of one and the same formula, but may also consist in the mutual recognition of different formulas.

Having provided this personal view of divine providence concerning the formation of dogma, I now ask whether doctrinal understanding in the Church can be connected with the promise of Christ: "When the Spirit of truth comes, he will guide you into all the truth . . ." (John 16:13).

W. Hendriksen obviously thinks that the promise relates both to the apostles and later Church leaders. He states that the Holy Spirit:

> . . . exerts his influence upon the regenerated consciousness of the child of God (and here, in particular of the office-bearers) and enlarges upon the themes which were introduced by Jesus during his earthly sojourn. Thus, he guides into all the truth, that is, into the *whole* [with emphasis on this adjective] body of redemptive revelation. He never stresses one point of doctrine at the expense of all the others. (*Commentary*, 1954, p. 328)

Commenting on John 16:12–15, Bishop B. F. Westcott writes that:

> . . . this section distinctly marks the position of the apostles with regard to revelation as unique; and so also by implication the office of the apostolic writings as a record of their teaching.

The same trust which enables us to believe that the apostles were guided into the Truth, leads us also to believe that by the providential leading of the Spirit they were so guided as to present it in such a way that it might remain in a permanent form. (*Commentary*, 1924, p. 230)

In general agreement with Westcott, Raymond E. Brown adds the important comment that "the Paraclete's guidance along the way of all truth involves more than a deeper intellectual understanding of what Jesus has said—it involves a way of life in conformity with Jesus' teaching" (*Commentary*, 1966, p. 715). Regarding the last words in verse 13, "he will declare to you the things that are to come," the best interpretation appears to be that the Spirit will give understanding of the passion and resurrection of Jesus to the apostles. When Jesus spoke, the passion, cross, and resurrection were future events. Thus, I agree with both Westcott and Brown that this promise is for the apostles, and therefore has no direct application for the creation of doctrine within the Church in history. For the guidance of God in the formation of dogma by the Church, we have to appeal not to a specific promise but to the general doctrine of the Lordship of Christ over the Church. We believe that Christ, the Lord, is concerned with the totality of the life of his Church and that the formation of dogma is a part of this totality.

Thus, I generally agree with Hans Küng, who in *Infallible?* (1971) argues for the indefectibility instead of the traditional Roman Catholic idea of the infallibility of the Church in her holding of truth. By truth he does not mean a system of correct propositions but a knowledge of God in his revelation that maintains a living fellowship with Christ:

In the strict sense of the word, God alone is infallible. He alone is *a priori* free from error (*immunis ab errore*) in each and every instance. . . . But the Church which is composed of human beings, who are not and can never become God, can very humanly continually deceive itself and others at all levels and in all fields. For the avoidance of misunderstanding, it is better to ascribe to the Church, not 'infallibility', but on the basis of faith in the promises [e.g., Matt. 16:18], 'indefectibility' or 'perpetuity', indestructibility and imperishability; in short, a fundamental remaining in the truth in spite of all possible errors. (pp. 152–53)

Thus, we can be sure that God will never allow his Church and his truth to disappear from human history. They will remain part of the human scene until the end of time.

Confessions of Faith

When I discuss the development of doctrine with seminarians, two questions concerning creeds usually arise: do Protestant churches need new confessions for today, and is it correct to translate a Protestant Confession into a "third-world" language to become the doctrinal basis of a young church?

With regard to the first question, it is my conviction that the principle of a book of confessions is a good one. I believe that each major denomination should produce a contemporary confession of faith which should be brief and cover only the major points of the Faith. This would be placed with those other confessions or theological statements which represent its doctrinal tradition in a book of documents. Such a production would have the effect of shifting the emphasis towards a twentieth-century rather than a sixteenth- or seventeenth-century expression of doctrine. It is to be hoped that there would be fewer differences in the modern confessions than in some of the older ones. Therefore, the basis for dialogue between different traditions/ denominations would not be difficult to find. This dialogue is surely necessary. If we have one God, one Faith, and one hope, then we must work towards either an agreement in doctrine or towards an agreement that our different doctrines are not mutually exclusive.

Now I fully recognize that many problems are raised by this proposal. For example, it is claimed that in "liberal" denominations the new confessions would be considered inadequate because they are likely to proceed from a low view of Scripture. There is some force to this observation, but until we have seen the end products we cannot know. Even so, certain evangelical denominations could initiate a beginning. For example, the new Presbyterian Church of American (P.C.A.) and the older Lutheran Church—Missouri Synod could produce short, modern confessions. Then the two groups could meet and see how, in the same American culture and with the same Bible, they understand that Bible's doctrinal teaching today. Who knows where this kind of effort could lead? Although we need to be realistic and reckon with the kind of sin which hardens our hearts and clutters our minds with good reasons for the continuance of our separate existence and confessions, we must also strive to obtain that unity of the Church which all confess we have in Christ. Merely to talk of the "invisible Church" of which we are all members, and to claim that this invisible unity is all that God requires, is not acceptable. The logic of the evangelical commitment to an inspired, written Word of God is that there should be, in one culture and language, a general agreement by evangelicals regarding its doctrinal meaning. I do not believe that such an agreement yet exists.

To return to the basic question, I would add that, apart from the ecumenical aspects of the new confession, such a document is needed for other reasons. We need to state our beliefs in contemporary language so that Church members can understand what we teach, and the world can see that we do relate to the ideas and questions of today. God wishes to hear his people praising him in doctrines which truly represent our thinking and not merely that of our forefathers.

Regarding the second question, we have a duty to make converts, establish congregations, teach the Faith, and train leaders in missions. Also, we have a duty to provide (or help to provide) the young churches with the Scriptures in their language. We do not have a duty to export our architecture for their church buildings, our music for their worship, or our patterns of church attendance and activities for their church life. Teaching the Faith and particularly training leaders should include the teaching of doctrine. Does this mean that we have to translate, for example, the Belgic or Westminster Confession and make this their doctrinal standard? I hope not. By all means these creeds should be translated so church leaders may read them, but in addition, they should be explained as creeds that belong to a Western culture and creeds that were designed, at least in part, to answer questions which are only important in Western history. The Western confessions can serve as signposts to the church leaders, pointing them to the meaning of Scripture. If we are to insist on any dogma, then it should be the truly Catholic dogma of the Trinity, even though this is encapsuled in ancient Greek terms. We need to teach them how to do exegesis, and interpret the Bible as well as point out what the Western Church has regarded as important in Scripture. Yet, in the last analysis, we must pray that these trained leaders eventually will express the doctrines of the Faith in their own terms and that they will be faithful to the paradigm set by the apostolic interpretation of Christ. To force the divisions of our Western churches on people of a different history and culture is sinful and contrary to the paradigm of unity found in Christ.

EPILOGUE

I REALIZE that I have not asked all the questions that need to be asked regarding development of doctrine, and neither have I provided definitive answers to the questions I have asked. In part, at least, this is because my subject is exceedingly difficult. We have one Bible upon which many doctrinal traditions are based, and the relation of these traditions to the Bible is far from simple. My hope is that I will challenge and inspire theologically-educated men and women to assess their own traditions critically and then to work charitably and persuasively towards a greater understanding between the different traditions. Today, in evangelicalism, we do not need more "Luthers" to stand against the world and then go their own separate Lutheran, Calvinist, or Methodist ways. We need people who, seeing the divisions, also see the possibility of deeper and more practical unity in Christ.